FOR ORGANS, PIANOS & ELECTRONIC KEYBOARDS

E-Z PLAY TODAY

2

COUNTRY SOUND
5TH EDITION

T0034031

Always on My Mind 2

Back in the Saddle Again 4

Behind Closed Doors 6

Blue Bayou 8

Blue Eyes Crying in the Rain 14

Boot Scootin' Boogie 16

Could I Have This Dance 11

Crazy 20

Don't It Make My Brown Eyes Blue 22

El Paso 24

Folsom Prison Blues 32

For the Good Times 29

Forever And Ever, Amen 34

Friends in Low Places 39

Funny How Time Slips Away 42

Galveston 44

Gentle on My Mind 52

Green Green Grass of Home 56

Have I Told You Lately That I Love You 58

He Stopped Loving Her Today 60

Heartaches by the Number 62

Help Me Make It Through the Night 64

Hey, Good Lookin' 66

I Can't Stop Loving You 68

I Fall to Pieces 70

I Walk the Line 72

Jambalaya (On the Bayou) 74

Jolene 47

King of the Road 76

The Last Word in Lonesome Is Me 78

Make the World Go Away 80

Mama Tried 82

Mammas Don't Let Your Babies Grow
Up to Be Cowboys 86

Mountain Music 90

Oh, Lonesome Me 98

Okie from Muskogee 95

Stand by Your Man 102

Tennessee Waltz 104

(Smooth As) Tennessee Whiskey 108

Your Cheatin' Heart 106

ISBN 978-0-7935-1306-2

HAL•LEONARD®
CORPORATION
7777 W. BLUEMOUND RD. P.O. BOX 13819 MILWAUKEE, WI 53213

E-Z Play ® TODAY Music Notation © 1975 HAL LEONARD CORPORATION
E-Z PLAY and EASY ELECTRONIC KEYBOARD MUSIC are registered trademarks of HAL LEONARD CORPORATION

Always on My Mind

Registration 10
Rhythm: Ballad or Slow Rock

Words and Music by Wayne Thompson,
Mark James and Johnny Christopher

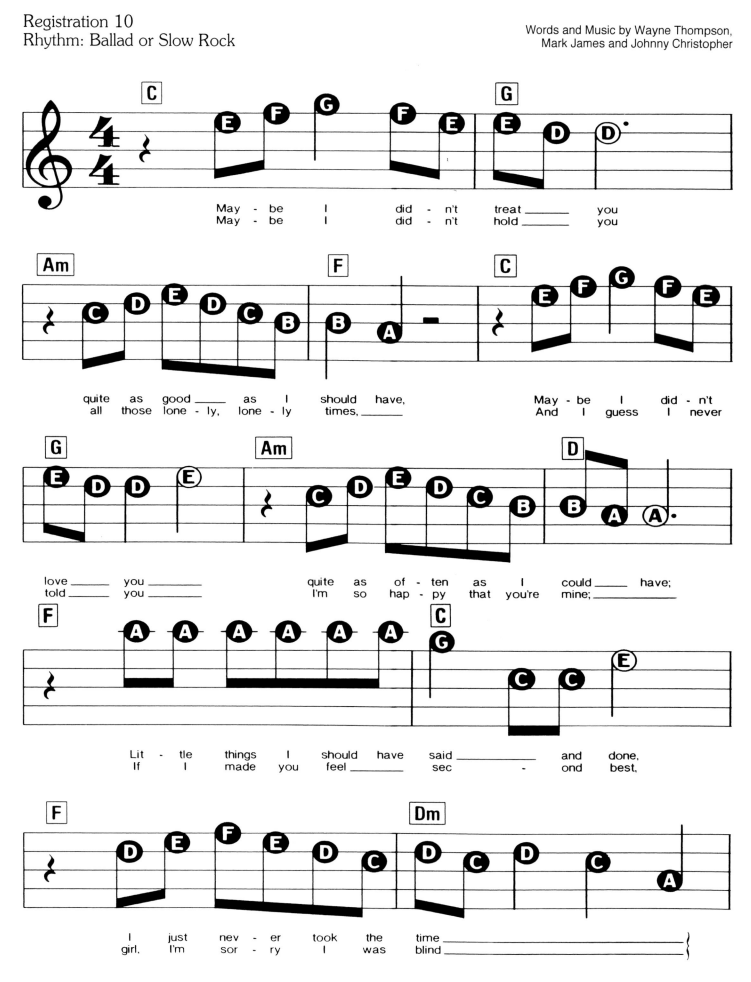

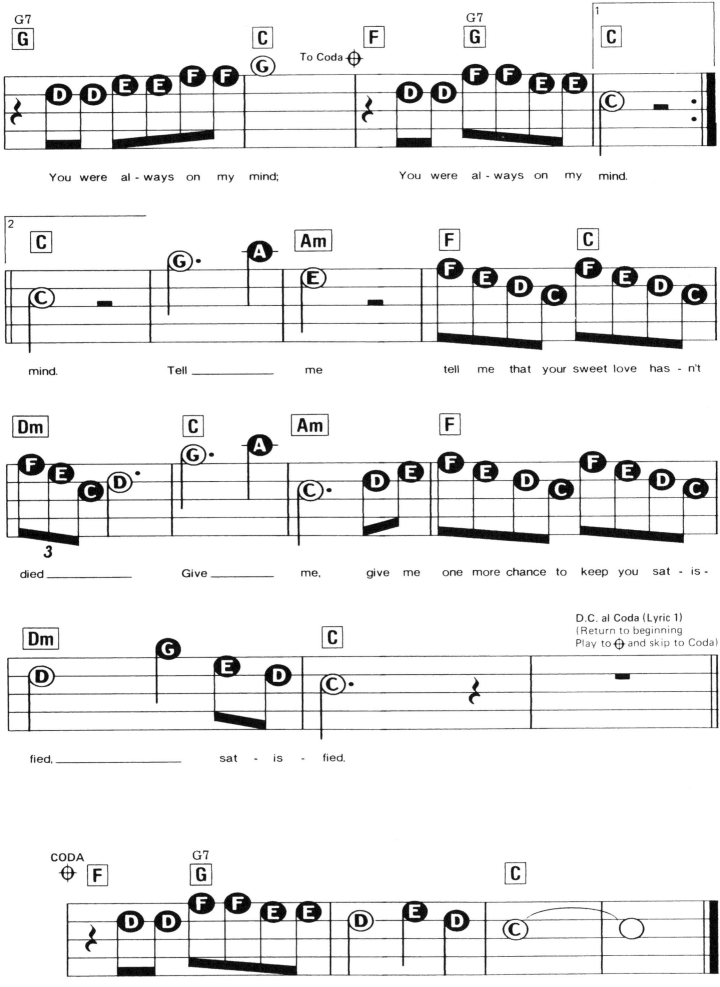

You were al-ways on my mind; You were al-ways on my mind.

mind. Tell _____ me tell me that your sweet love has-n't

died _____ Give _____ me, give me one more chance to keep you sat-is-

fied, _____ sat-is-fied.

You were al-ways on my mind._____

Back in the Saddle Again

Registration 1
Rhythm: Country Western or Fox Trot

Words and Music by Gene Autry
and Ray Whitley

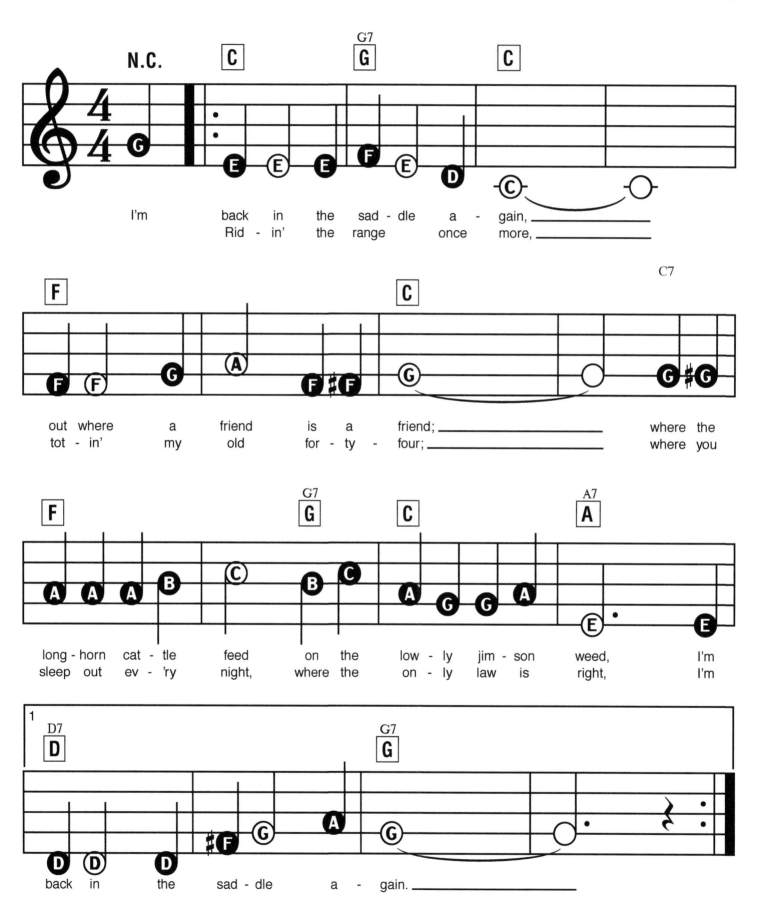

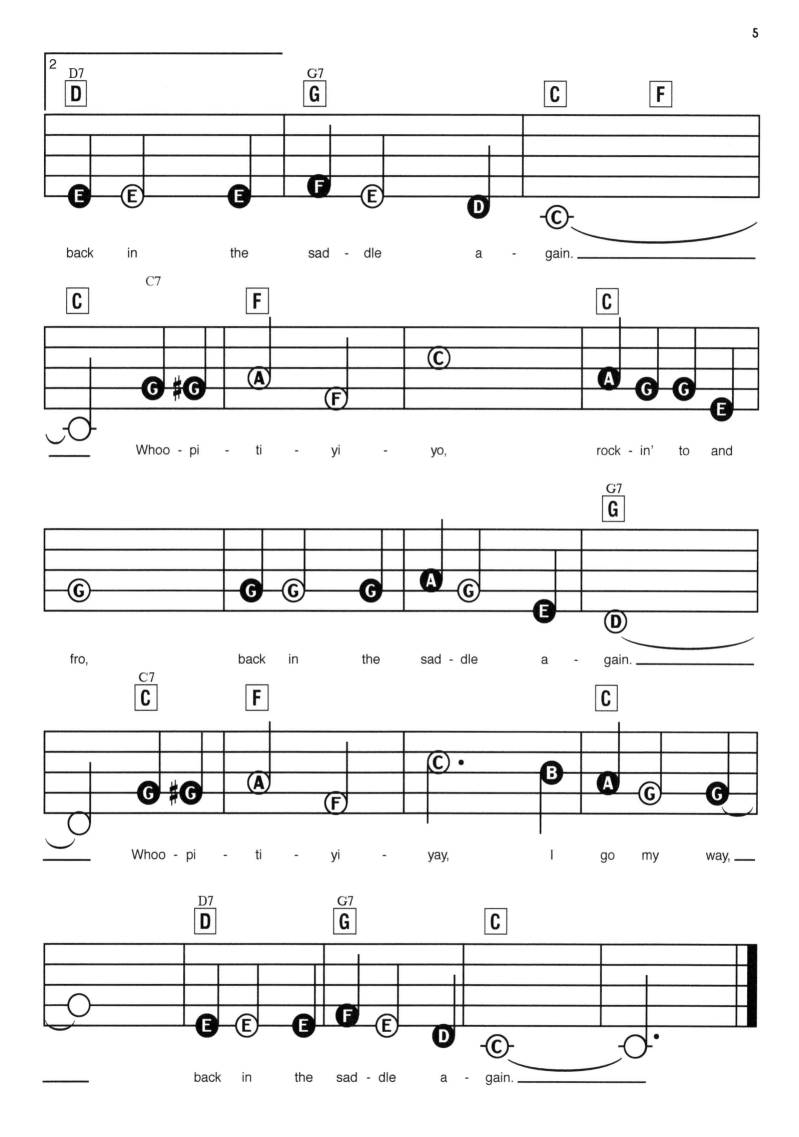

Behind Closed Doors

Registration 4
Rhythm: Country or Shuffle

Words and Music by
Kenny O'Dell

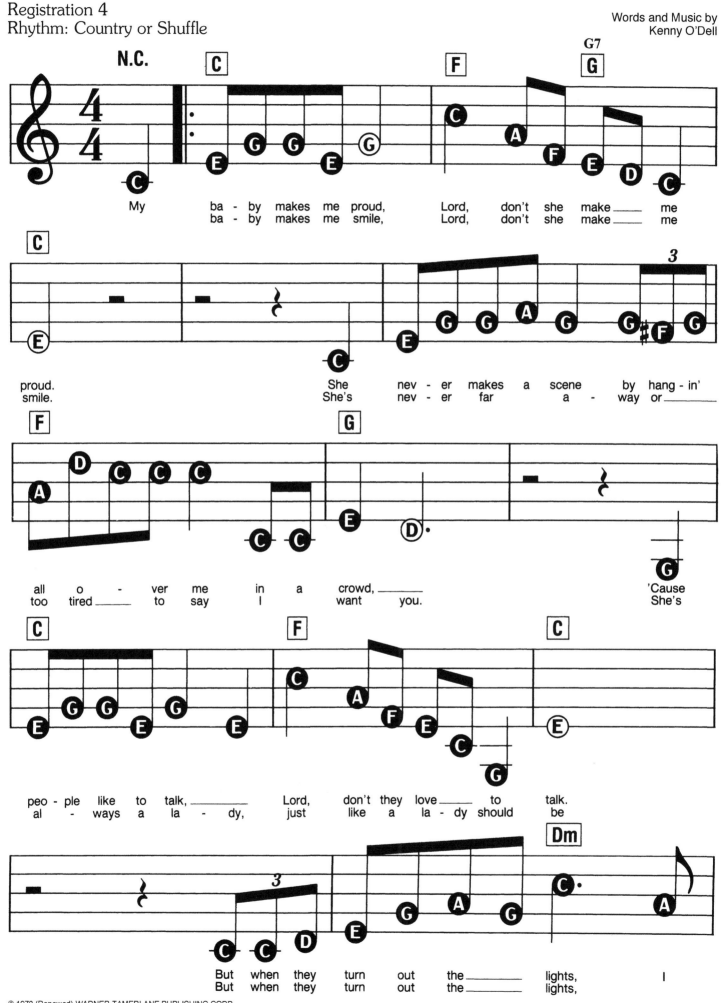

Blue Bayou

Registration 2
Rhythm: Rock or 8-Beat

Words and Music by Roy Orbison
and Joe Melson

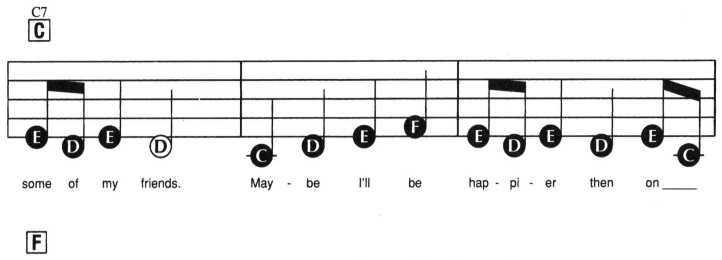

some of my friends. May - be I'll be hap - pi - er then on _____

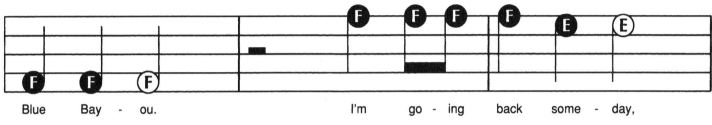

Blue Bay - ou. I'm go - ing back some - day,

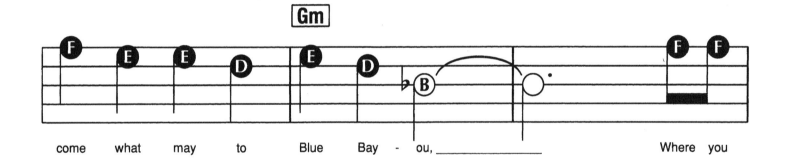

come what may to Blue Bay - ou, _____ Where you

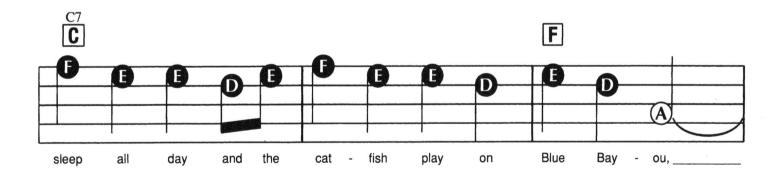

sleep all day and the cat - fish play on Blue Bay - ou, _____

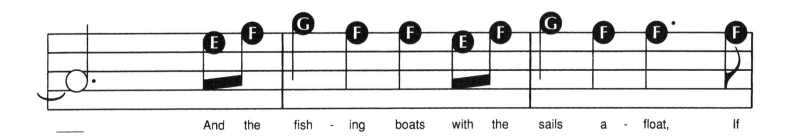

_____ And the fish - ing boats with the sails a - float, If

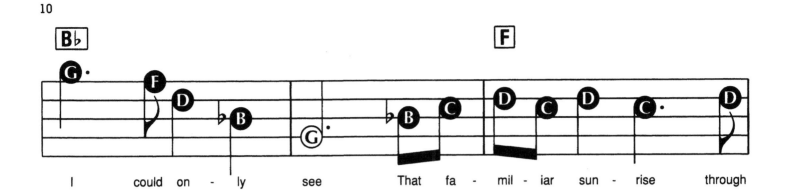

I could on - ly see That fa - mil - iar sun - rise through

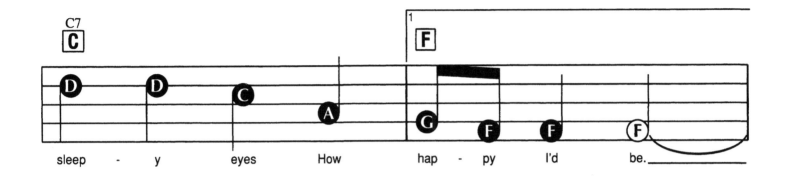

sleep - y eyes How hap - py I'd be. ____

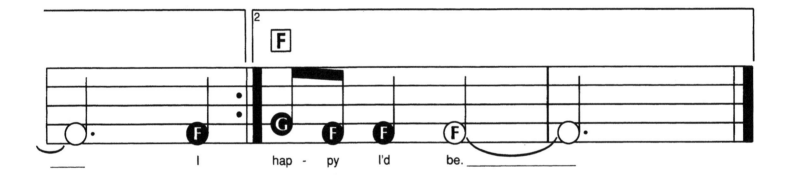

____ I hap - py I'd be. ____

Additional Lyrics

2nd Verse:

I feel so bad, I got a worried mind, I'm so lonely all the time
Since I left my baby behind on Blue Bayou
Saving nickles, saving dimes, working till the sun don't shine
Looking forward to happier times on Blue Bayou.

2nd Chorus

I'm going back someday, gonna stay on Blue Bayou
Where my folks I'll find, all the time on Blue Bayou
With that girl of mine by my side till the moon in the evening dies
Oh, some sweet day, gonna take away this hurtin' inside.

Could I Have This Dance
from URBAN COWBOY

Registration 4
Rhythm: Waltz

Words and Music by Wayland Holyfield
and Bob House

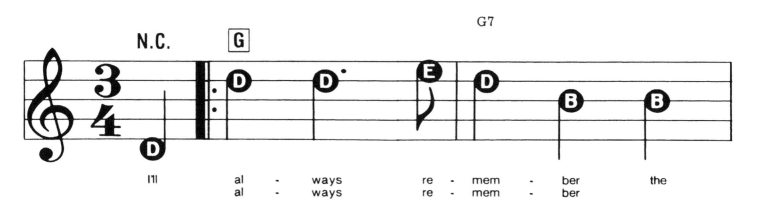

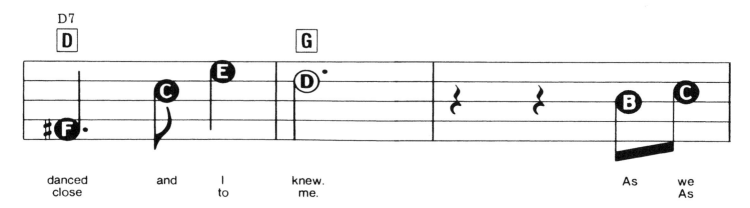

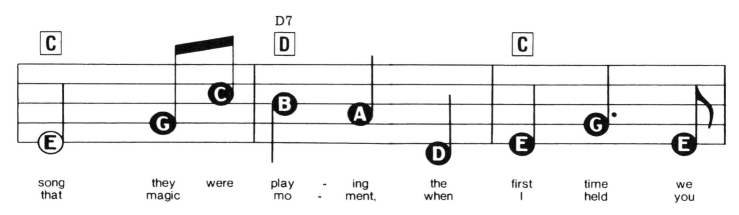

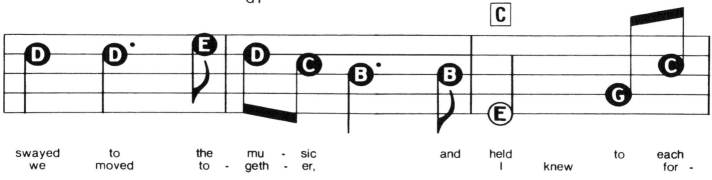

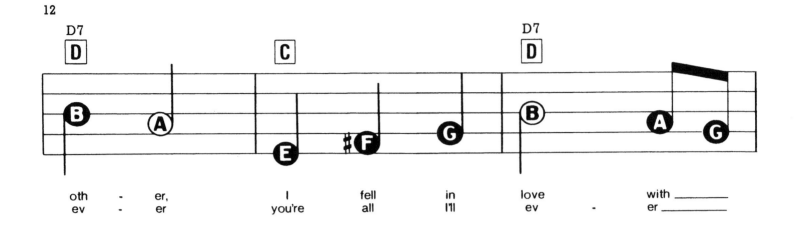

oth - er,
ev - er

I fell in love with _____
you're all I'll ev - er _____

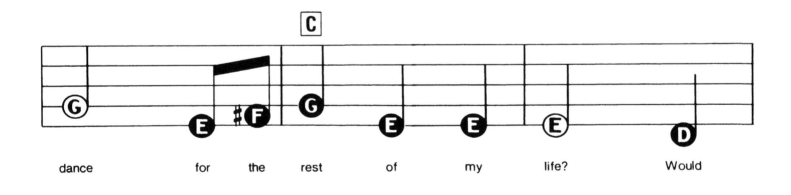

you.
need.

Could I have this

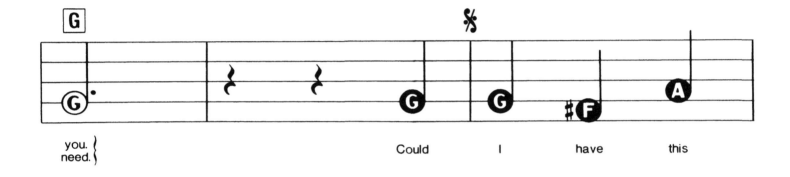

dance for the rest of my life? Would

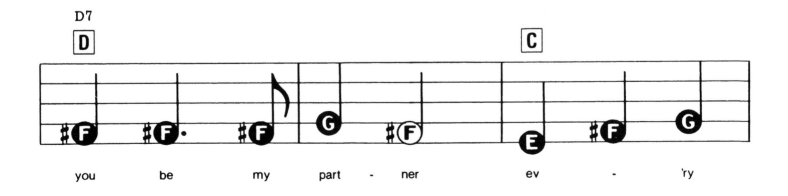

you be my part - ner ev - 'ry

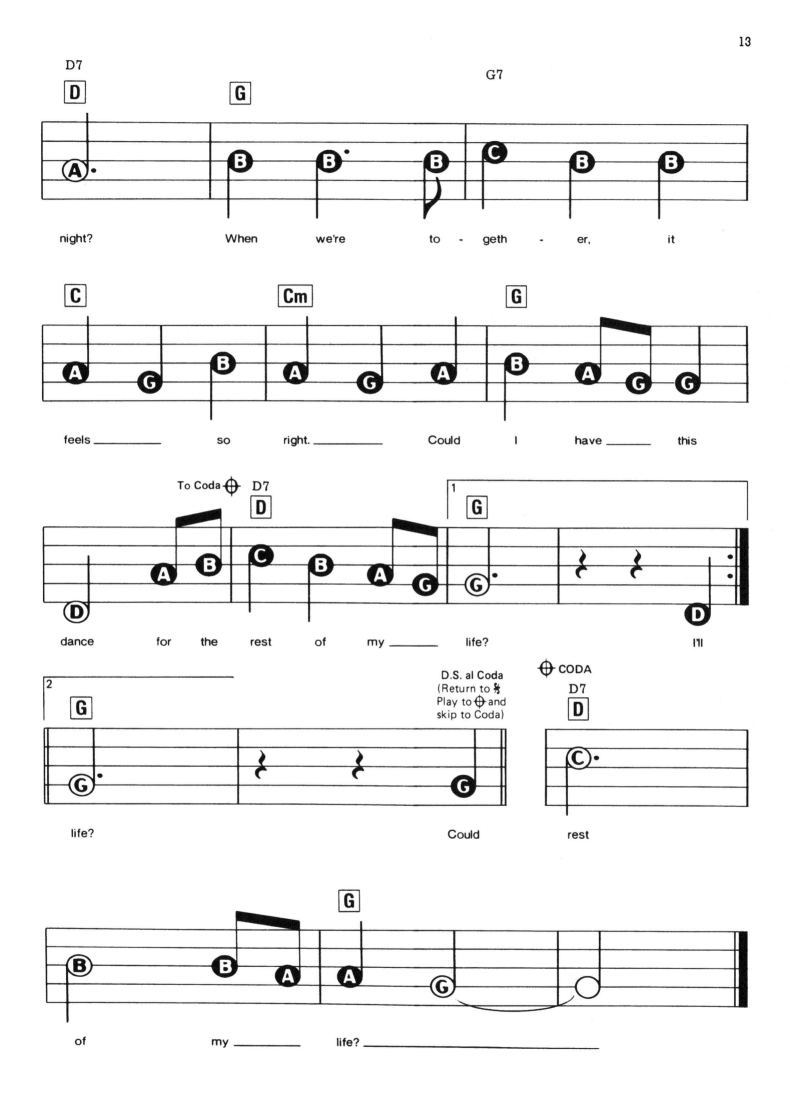

Blue Eyes Crying in the Rain

Registration 9
Rhythm: Swing or Country

Words and Music by
Fred Rose

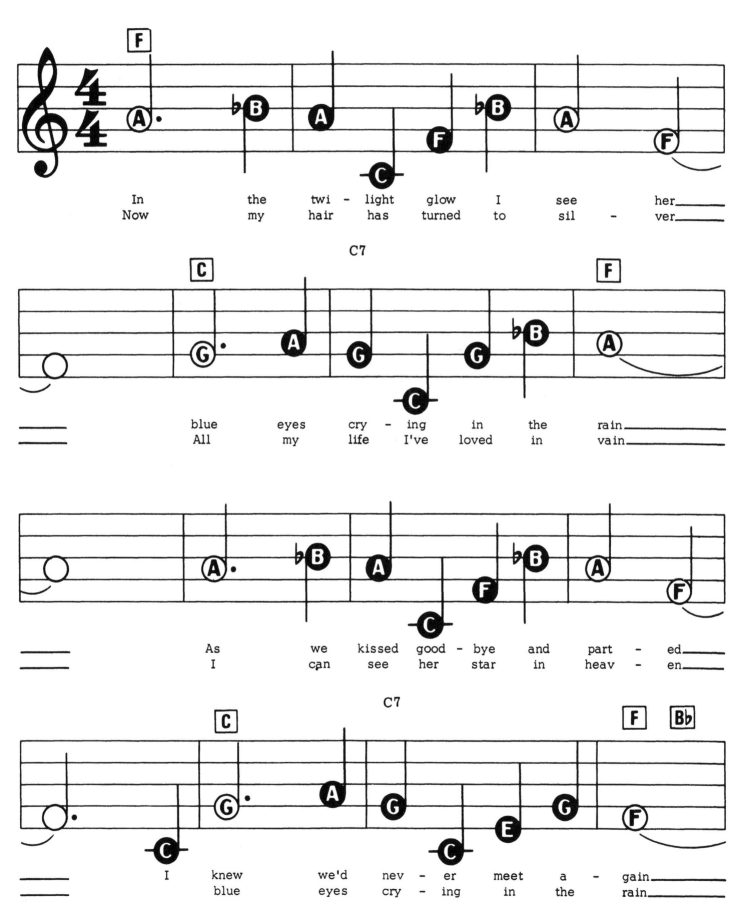

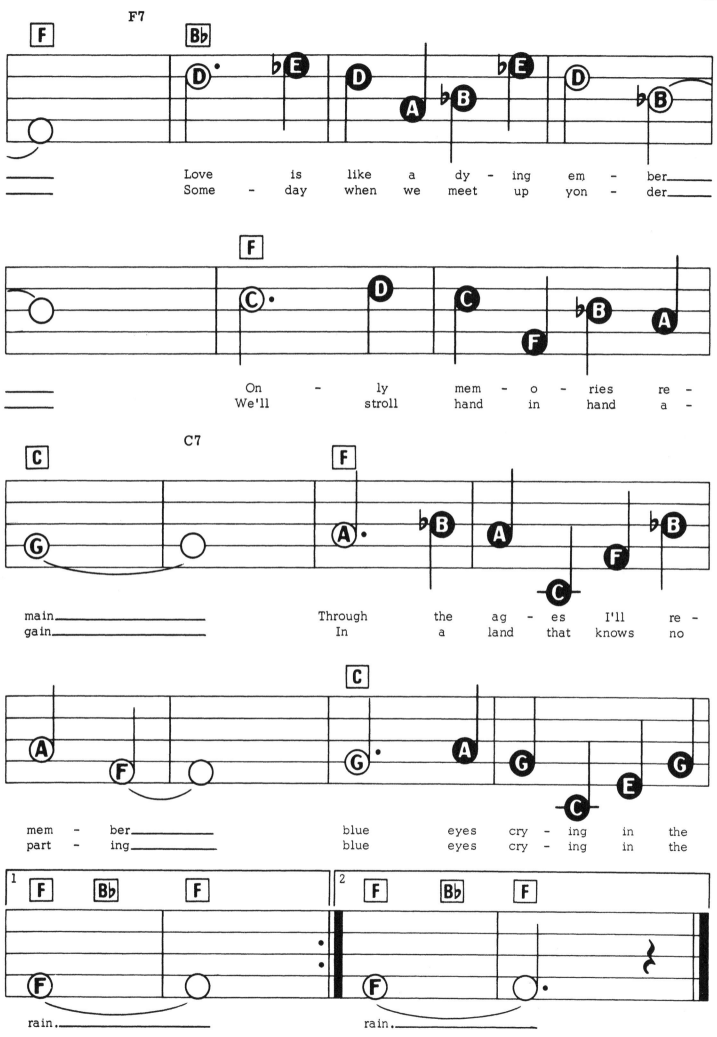

Boot Scootin' Boogie

Registration 2
Rhythm: Swing or Country Shuffle

Words and Music by
Ronnie Dunn

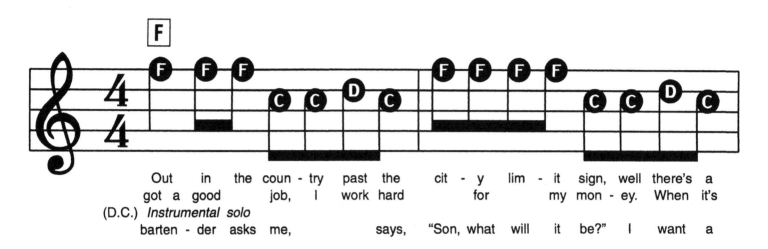

Out in the coun - try past the cit - y lim - it sign, well there's a
got a good job, I work hard for my mon - ey. When it's
(D.C.) *Instrumental solo*
barten - der asks me, says, "Son, what will it be?" I want a

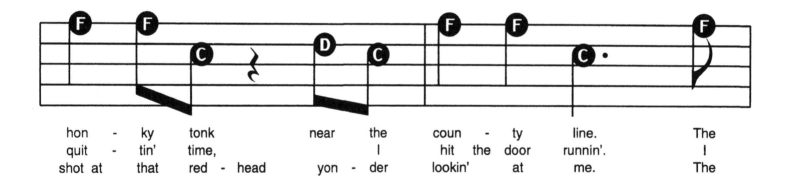

hon - ky tonk near the coun - ty line. The
quit - tin' time, I hit the door runnin'. I
shot at that red - head yon - der lookin' at me. The

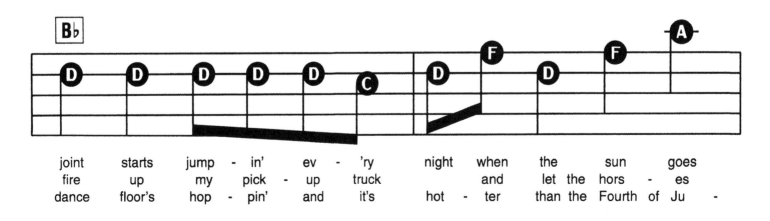

joint starts jump - in' ev - 'ry night when the sun goes
fire up my pick - up truck and let the hors - es
dance floor's hop - pin' and it's hot - ter than the Fourth of Ju -

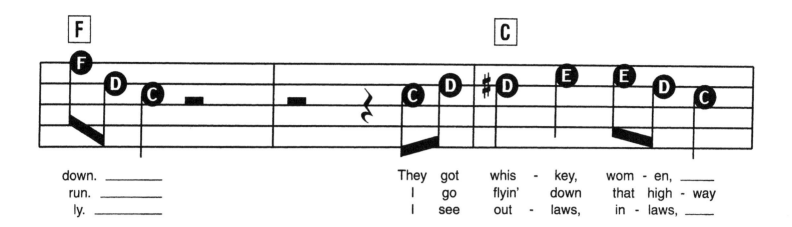

down. _____
run. _____
ly. _____

They got whis - key, wom - en, _____
I go flyin' down that high - way
I see out - laws, in - laws, _____

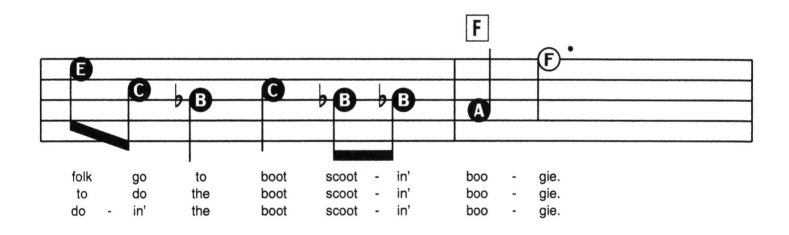

mu - sic and smoke. _____
to that hide - a - way _____
crooks and straights _____

It's where all the cow - boy
stuck out in the woods,
all out mak - in' it shake

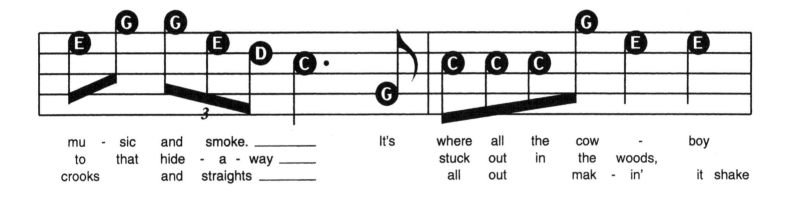

folk go to boot scoot - in' boo - gie.
to do the boot scoot - in' boo - gie.
do - in' the boot scoot - in' boo - gie.

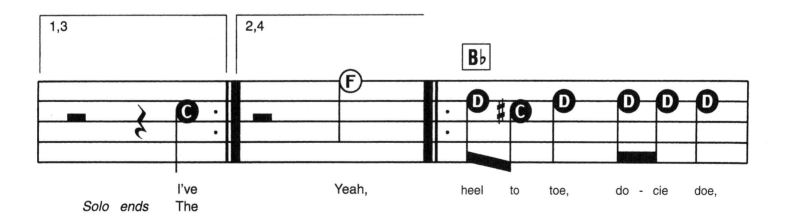

1,3

I've
Solo ends The

2,4

Yeah, heel to toe, do - cie doe,

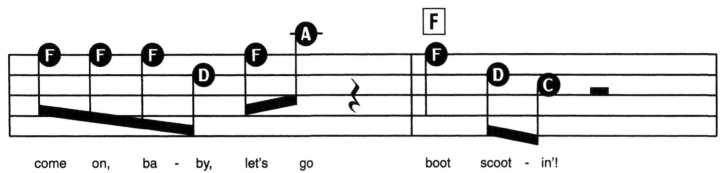

come on, ba - by, let's go boot scoot - in'!

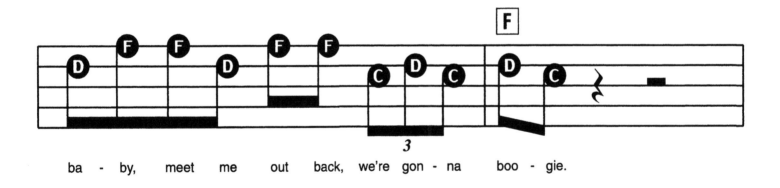

Whoa, Cad - il - lac, Black - jack,

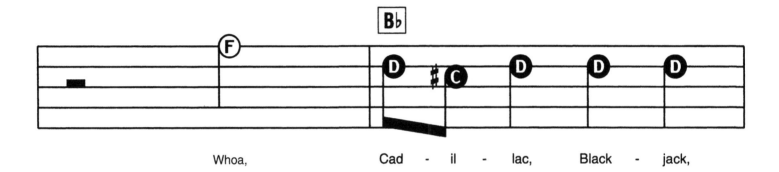

ba - by, meet me out back, we're gon - na boo - gie.

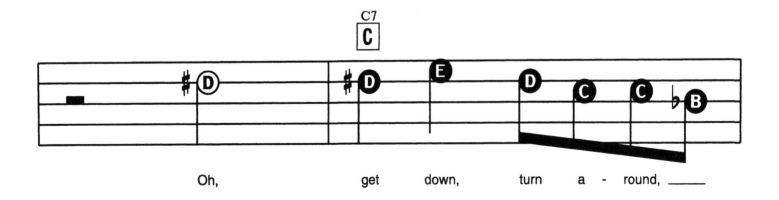

Oh, get down, turn a - round, _____

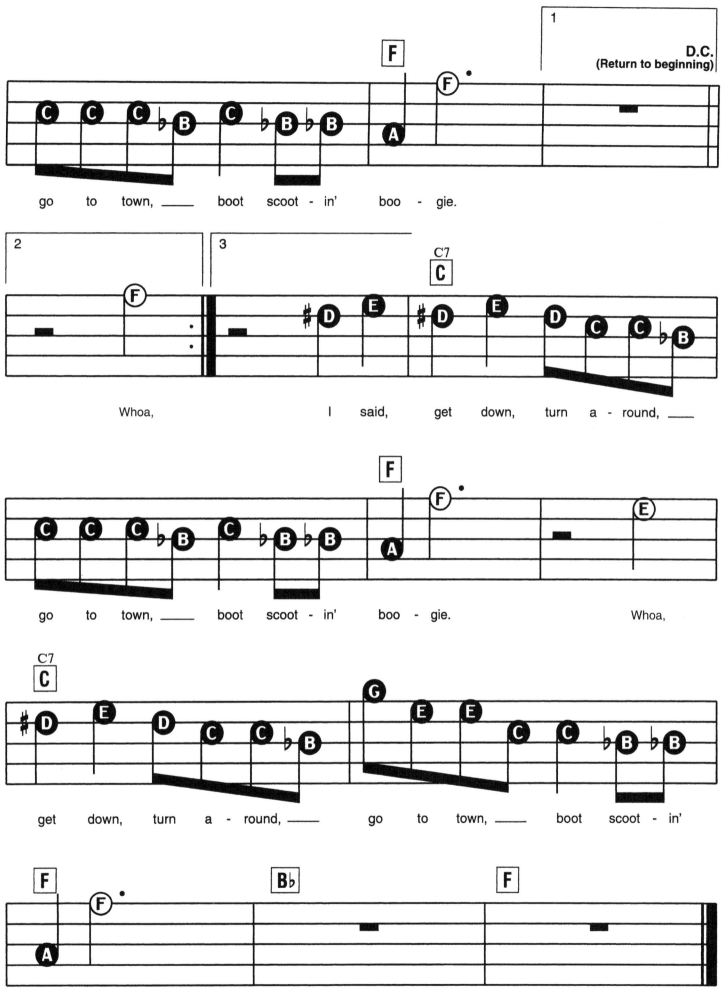

go to town, _____ boot scoot - in' boo - gie.

Whoa, I said, get down, turn a - round, _____

go to town, _____ boot scoot - in' boo - gie. Whoa,

get down, turn a - round, _____ go to town, _____ boot scoot - in'

boo - gie.

Crazy

Registration 2
Rhythm: Country or Ballad

Words and Music by
Willie Nelson

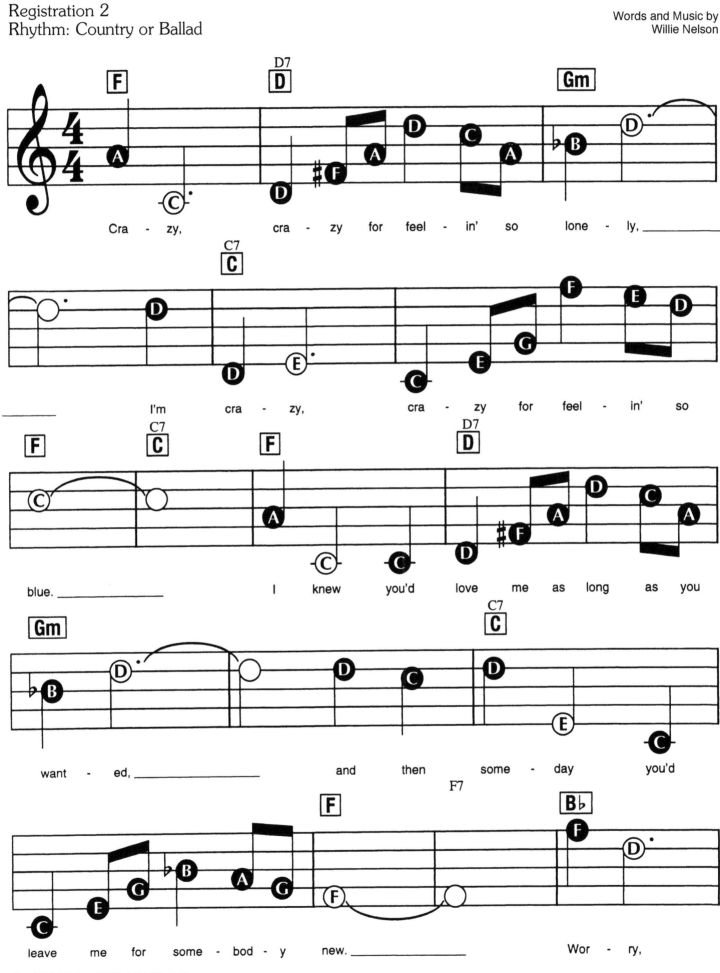

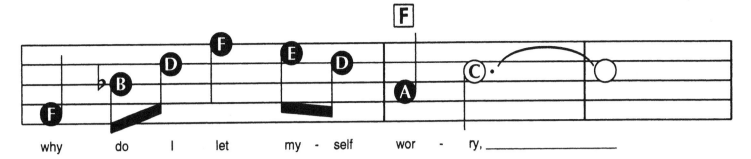

why do I let my-self wor - ry, _____

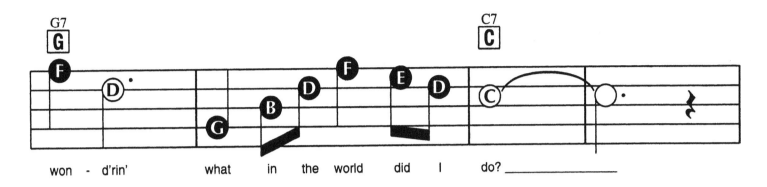

won - d'rin' what in the world did I do? _____

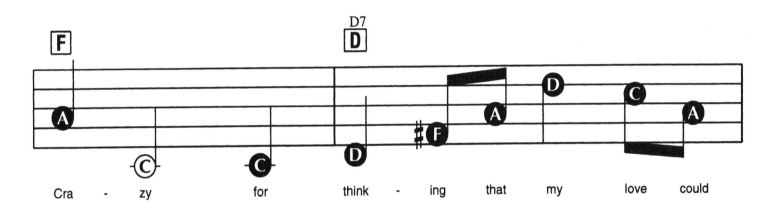

Cra - zy for think - ing that my love could

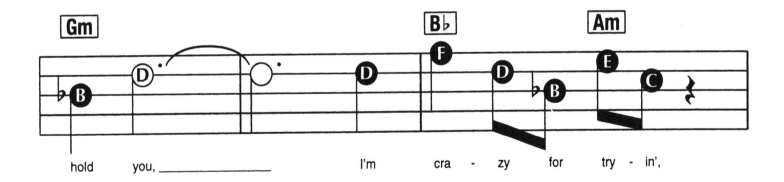

hold you, _____ I'm cra - zy for try - in',

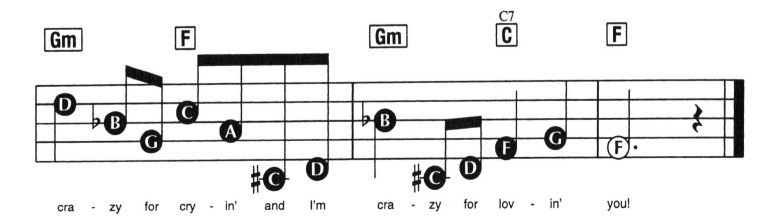

cra - zy for cry - in' and I'm cra - zy for lov - in' you!

Don't It Make My Brown Eyes Blue

Registration 2
Rhythm: Country Western or Ballad

Words and Music by
Richard Leigh

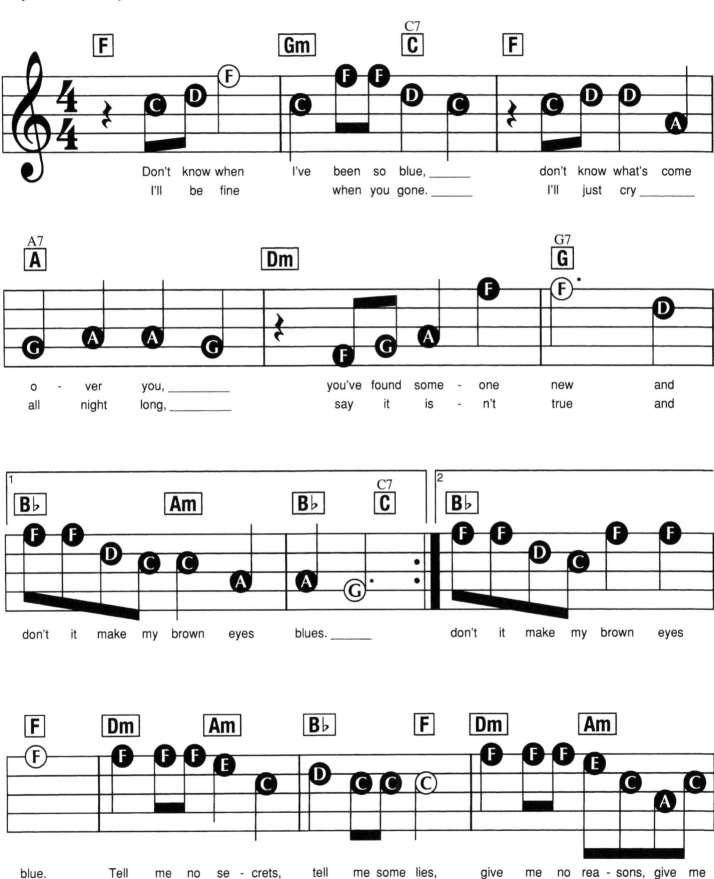

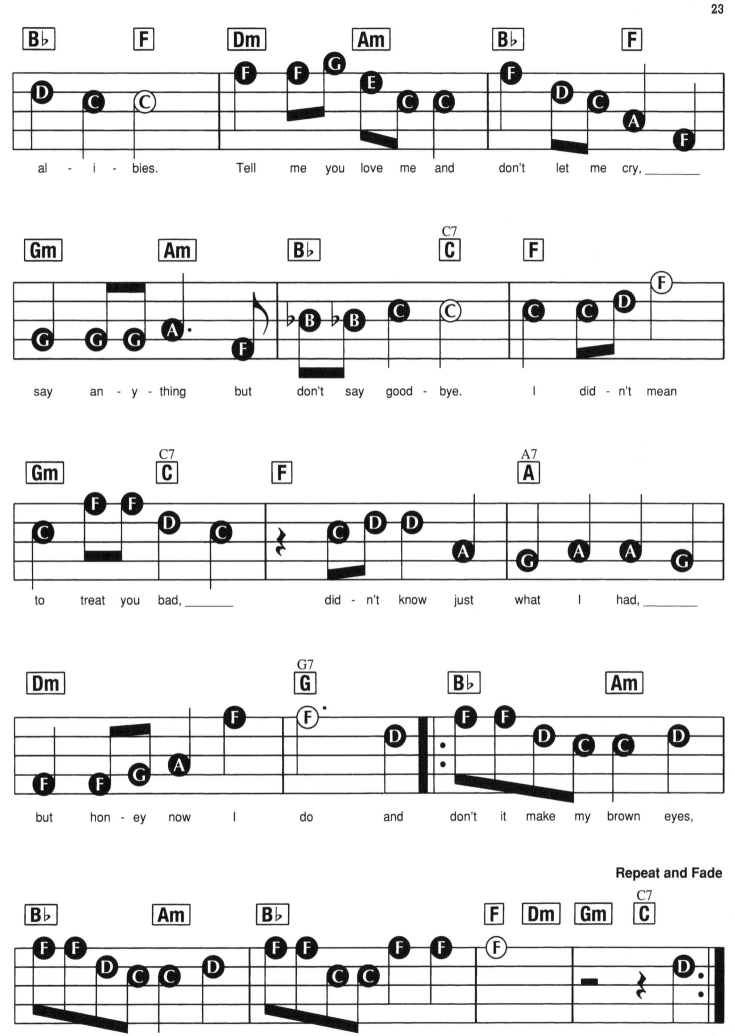

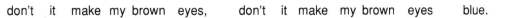

El Paso

Registration 5
Rhythm: Waltz

Words and Music by
Marty Robbins

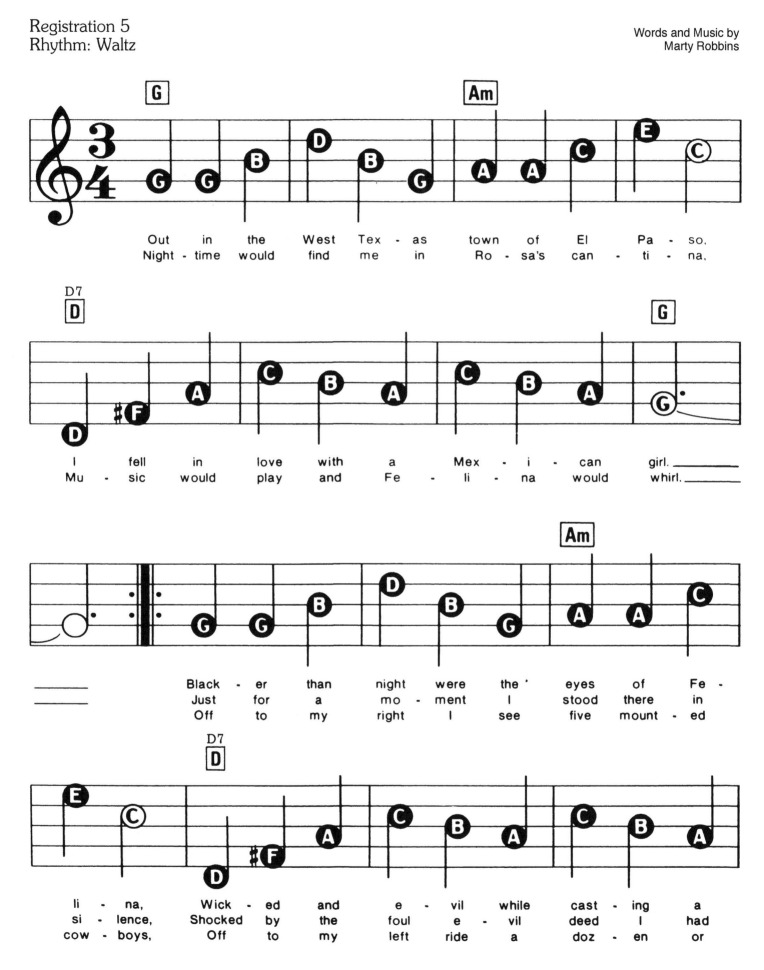

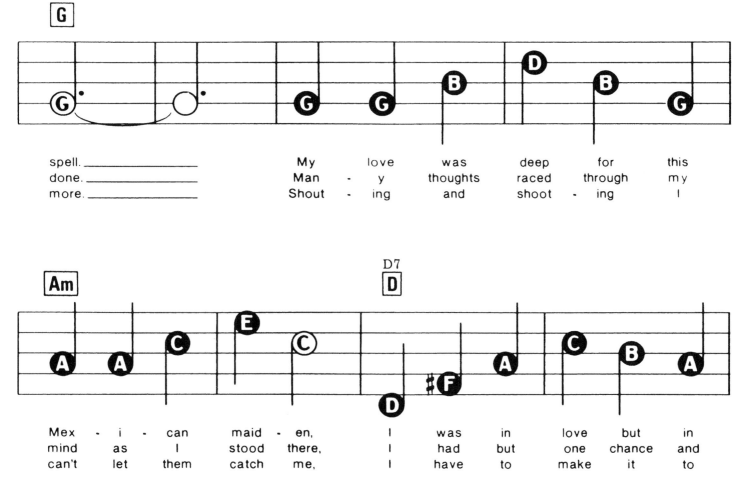

G

spell. _____
done. _____
more. _____

My love was deep for this
Man - y thoughts raced through my
Shout - ing and shoot - ing I

Am   D7 **D**

Mex - i - can maid - en, I was in love but in
mind as I stood there, I had but one chance in and
can't let them catch me, I have to make it to

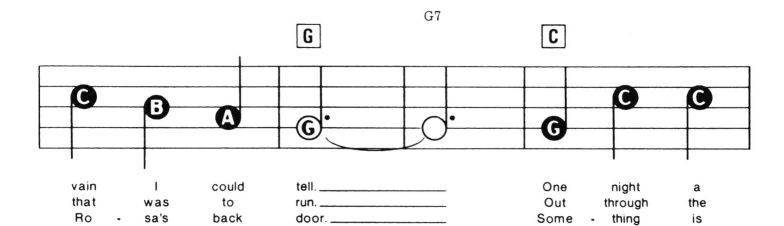

G7 **G**   **C**

vain I could tell. _____ One night a
that was to run. _____ Out through the
Ro - sa's back door. _____ Some - thing is

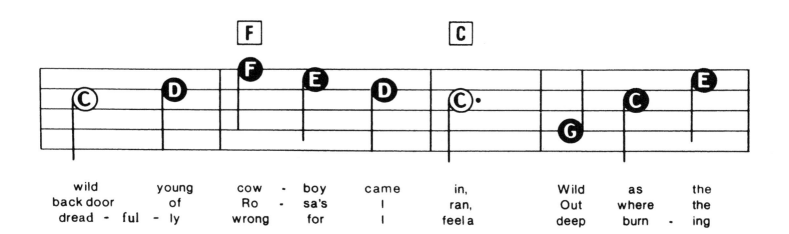

F   **C**

wild young cow - boy came in, Wild as the
back door of Ro - sa's I ran, Out where the
dread - ful - ly wrong for I feel a deep burn - ing

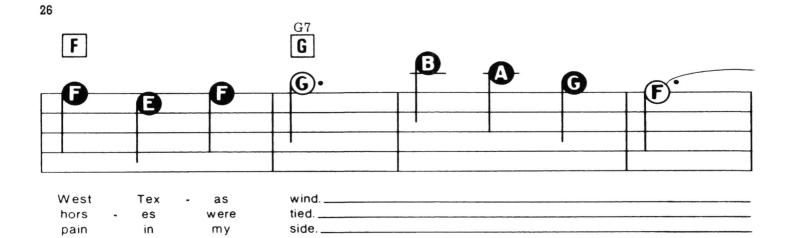

West Tex - as wind.
hors - es were tied.
pain in my side.

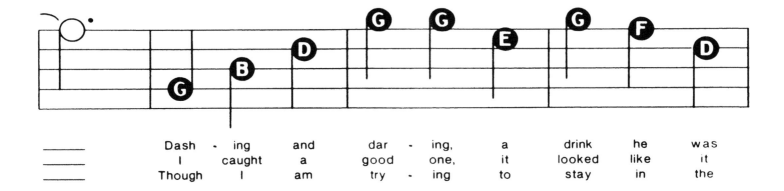

_____ Dash - ing and dar - ing, a drink he was
_____ I caught a good one, it looked like it
_____ Though I am try - ing to stay in the

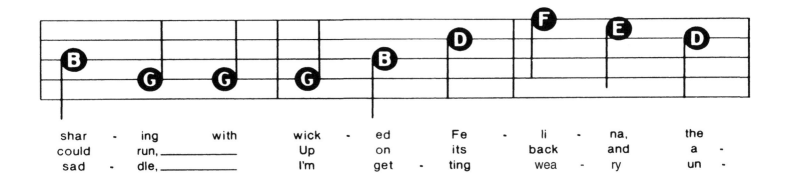

shar - ing with wick - ed Fe - li - na, the
could run, _____ Up on its back and a -
sad - dle, _____ I'm get - ting wea - ry un -

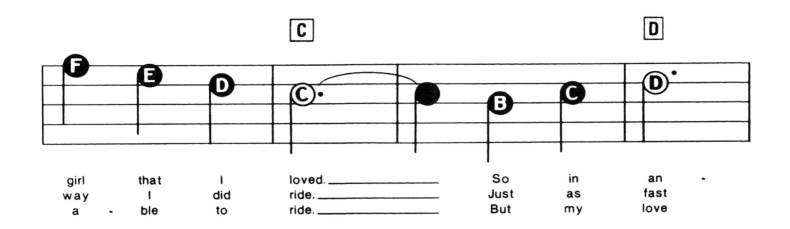

girl that I loved. _____ So in an -
way I did ride. _____ Just as fast
a - ble to ride. _____ But my love

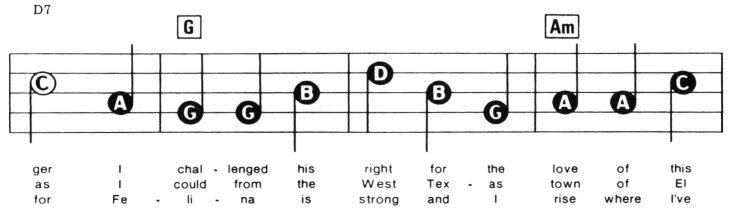

ger	I	chal - lenged	his	right	for	the	love	of	this
as	I	could	from	the	West	Tex - as	town	of	El
for	Fe - li - na	is	strong	and	I	rise	where	I've

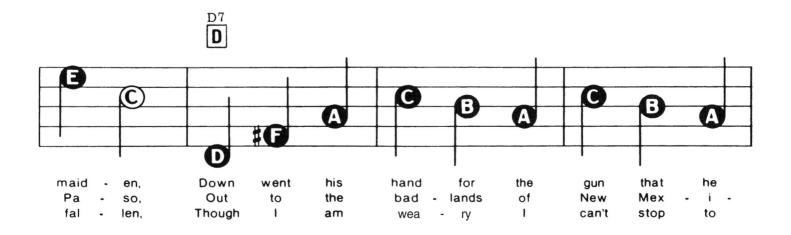

maid - en,	Down	went	his	hand	for	the	gun	that	he
Pa - so,	Out	to	the	bad - lands	of	New	Mex - i -
fal - len,	Though	I	am	wea - ry	I	can't	stop	to

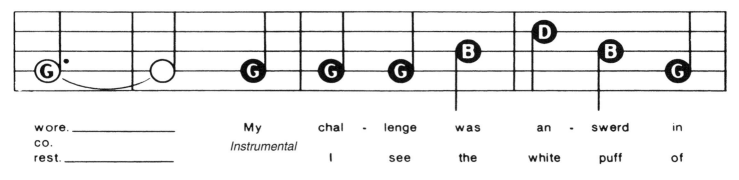

wore. _____	My	chal - lenge	was	an - swerd	in
co. _____	*Instrumental*
rest. _____	I	see	the	white	puff	of

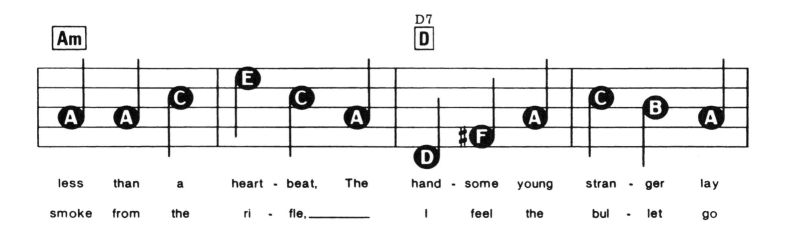

| less | than | a | heart - beat, | The | hand - some | young | stran - ger | lay |
| smoke | from | the | ri - fle, _____ | I | feel | the | bul - let | go |

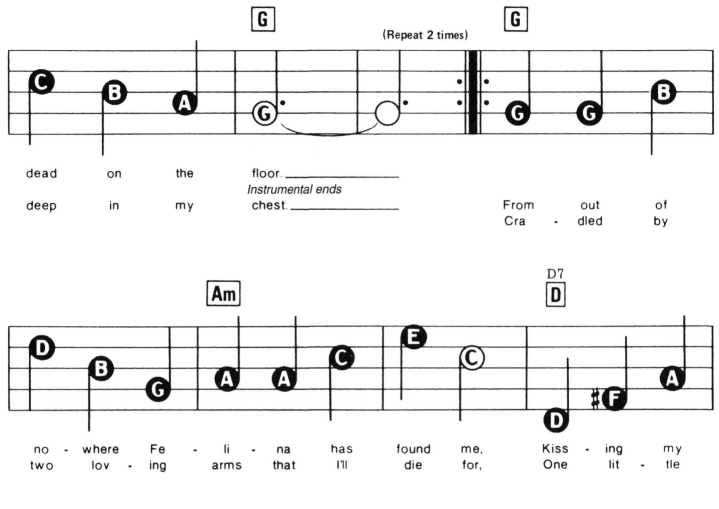

dead   on   the   floor._____

Instrumental ends

deep   in   my   chest._____   From   out   of

Cra - dled   by

no - where   Fe - li - na   has   found   me,   Kiss - ing   my

two   lov - ing   arms   that   I'll   die   for,   One   lit - tle

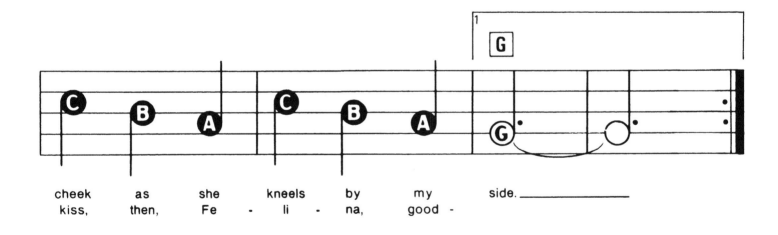

cheek   as   she   kneels   by   my   side._____

kiss,   then,   Fe - li - na,   my   good -

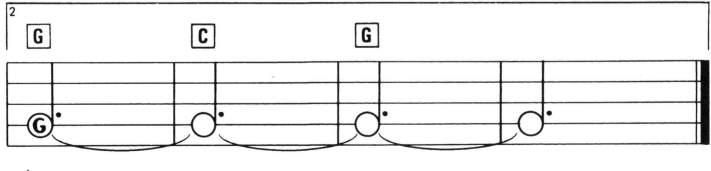

bye._____

For the Good Times

Registration 2
Rhythm: Country or Swing

Words and Music by
Kris Kristofferson

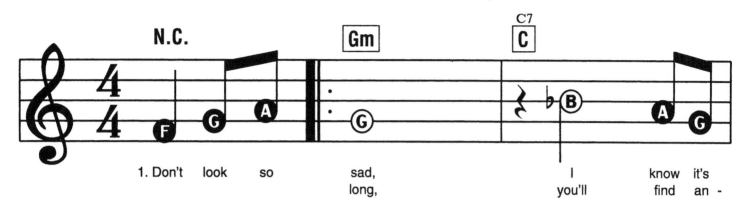

1. Don't look so sad,
long,

I know it's
you'll find an -

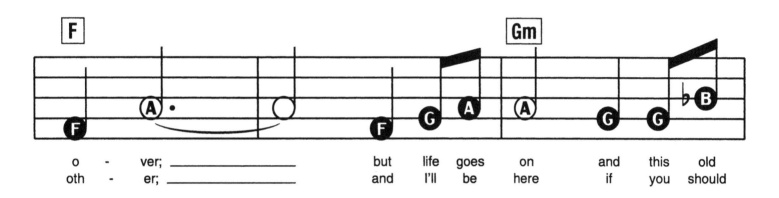

o - ver; _____
oth - er; _____

but life goes on and this old
and I'll be here if you should

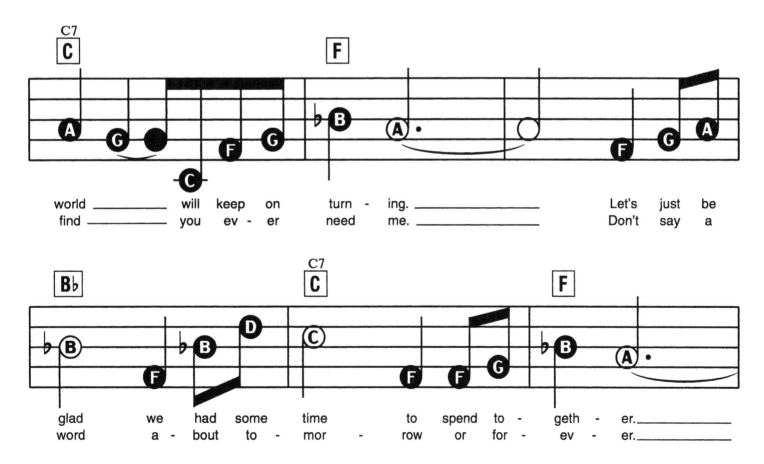

world _____ will keep on turn - ing. _____
find _____ you ev - er need me. _____

Let's just be
Don't say a

glad we had some time to spend to - geth - er. _____
word a - bout to - mor - row or for - ev - er. _____

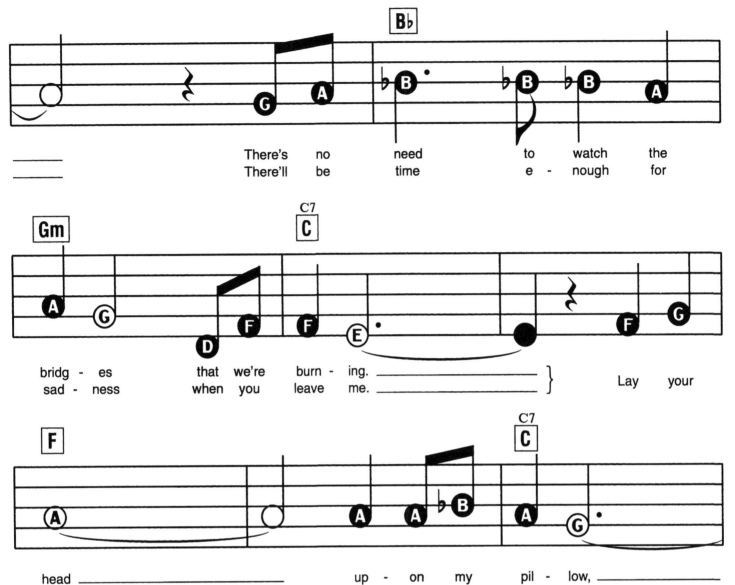

There's no | need | to | watch | the
There'll be | time | e - | nough | for

bridg - es | that | we're | burn - ing. _____ } Lay your
sad - ness | when | you | leave | me. _____

head _____ | up - on | my | pil - low, _____

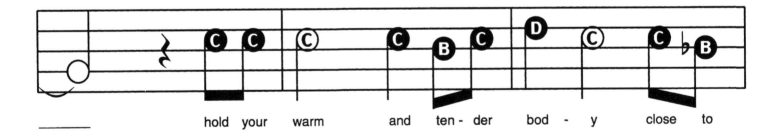

_____ hold your | warm | and | ten - der | bod - y | close | to

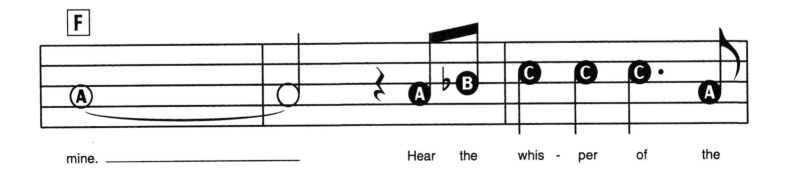

mine. _____ | Hear | the | whis - per | of | the

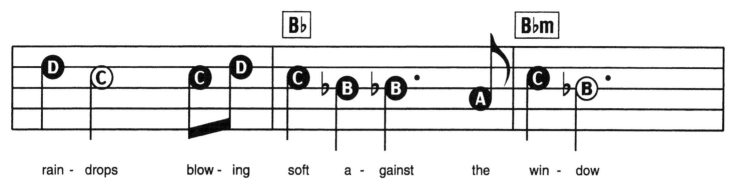

rain - drops blow - ing soft a - gainst the win - dow

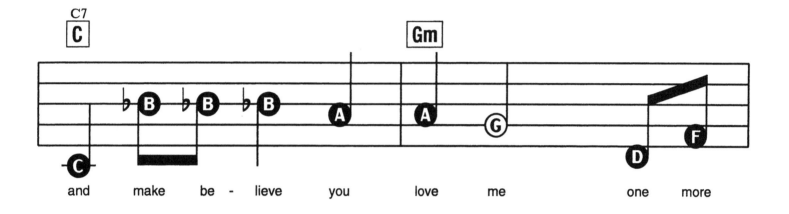

and make be - lieve you love me one more

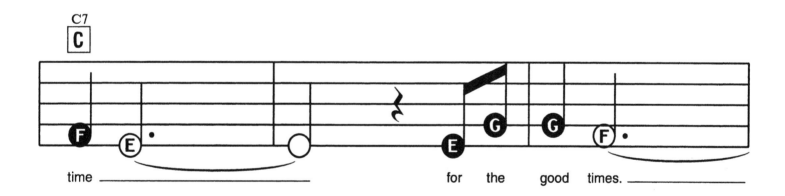

time _____ for the good times. _____

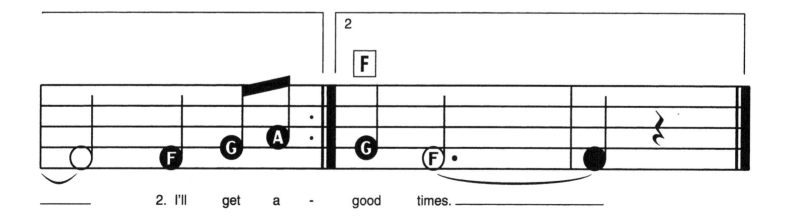

_____ 2. I'll get a - good times. _____

Folsom Prison Blues

Registration 3
Rhythm: Rock or Fox Trot

Words and Music by
John R. Cash

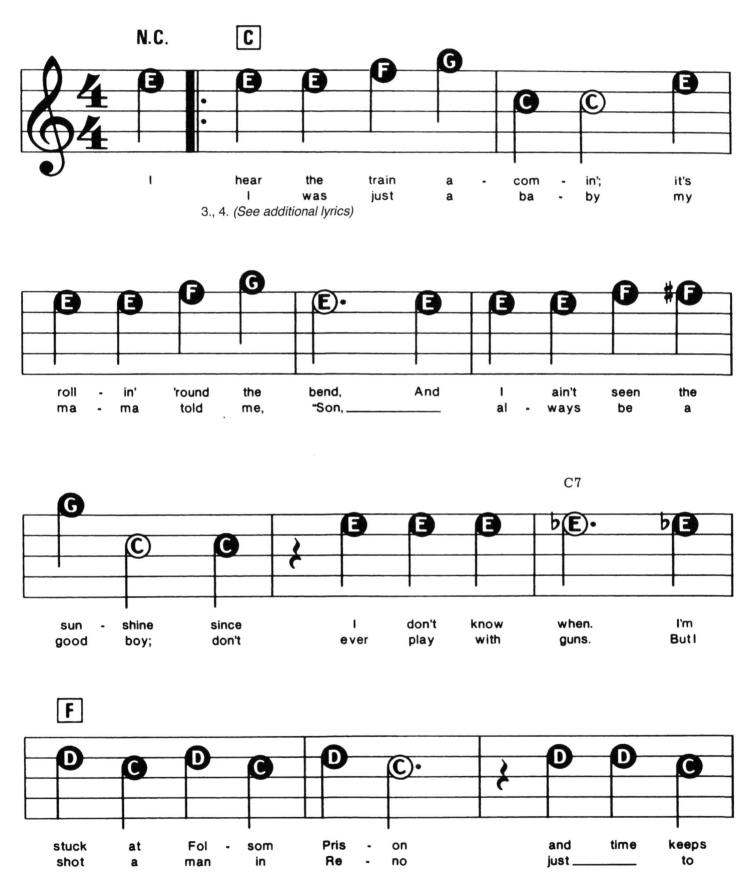

3., 4. *(See additional lyrics)*

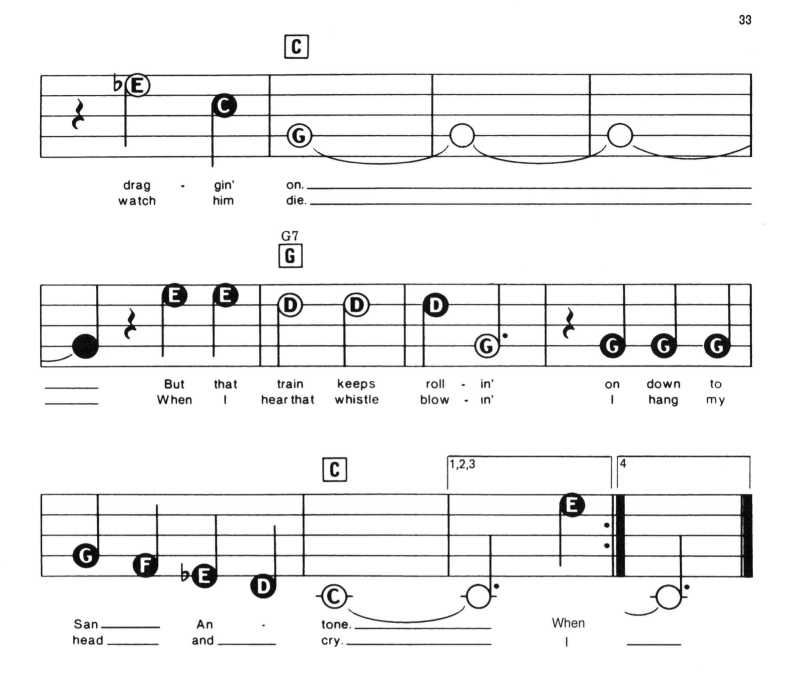

Additional Lyrics

3. I bet there's rich folks eatin' in a fancy dining car.
   They're prob'ly drinkin' coffee and smokin' big cigars,
   But I know I had it comin', I know I can't be free,
   But those people keep a-movin', and that's what tortures me.

4. Well, if they freed me from this prison, if that railroad train was mine,
   I bet I'd move over a little farther down the line,
   Far from Folsom Prison, that's where I want to stay.
   And I'd let that lonesome whistle blow my blues away.

Forever and Ever, Amen

Registration 4
Rhythm: Country

Words and Music by Paul Overstreet
and Don Schlitz

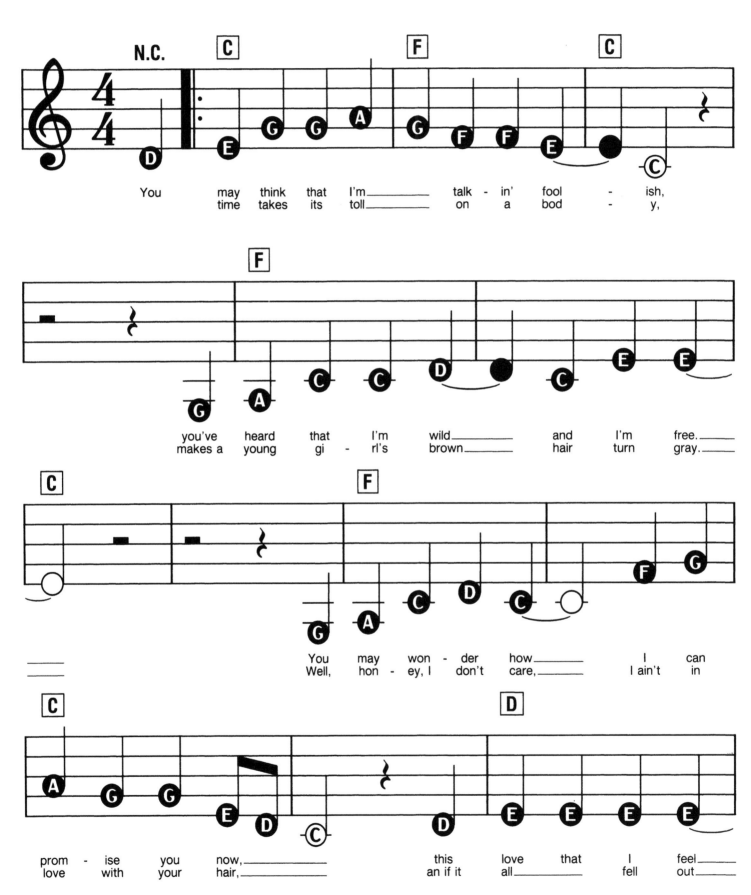

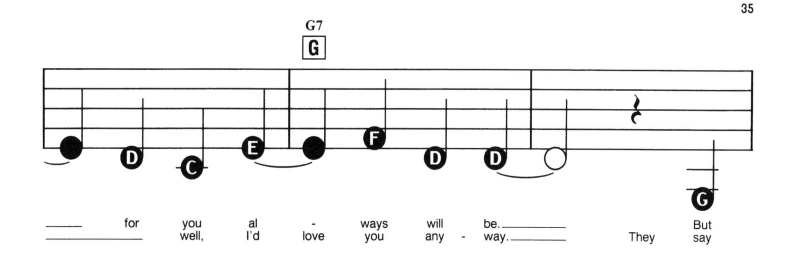

G7

| | | for | you | al | - | ways | will | be.____ | | They | But say |

____ well, I'd love you any - way.____

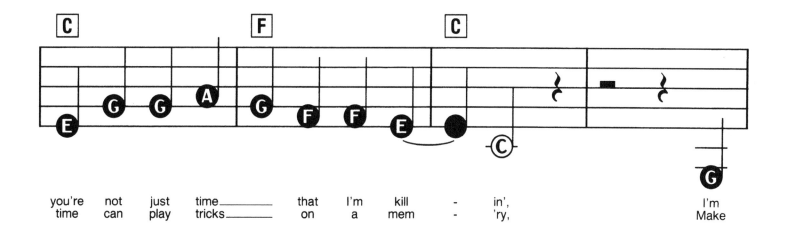

C   F   C

you're not just time____ that I'm kill - in',   I'm
time can just play tricks____ on a mem - 'ry,   Make

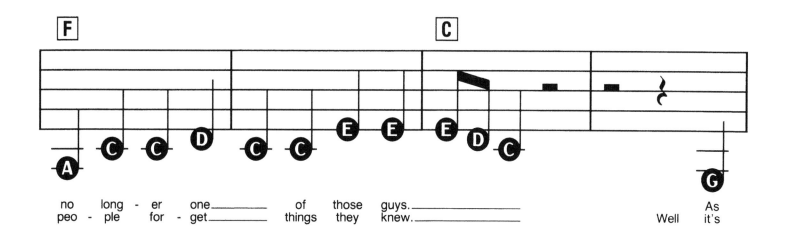

F   C

no long - er one____ of those guys.____   As
peo - ple for - get____ things they knew.____   Well it's

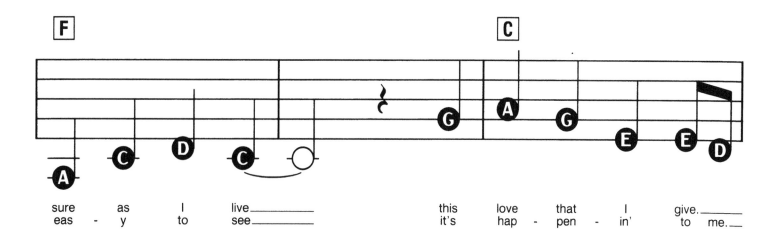

F   C

sure as I live____   this love that I give.____
eas - y to see____   it's hap - pen - in' to me.____

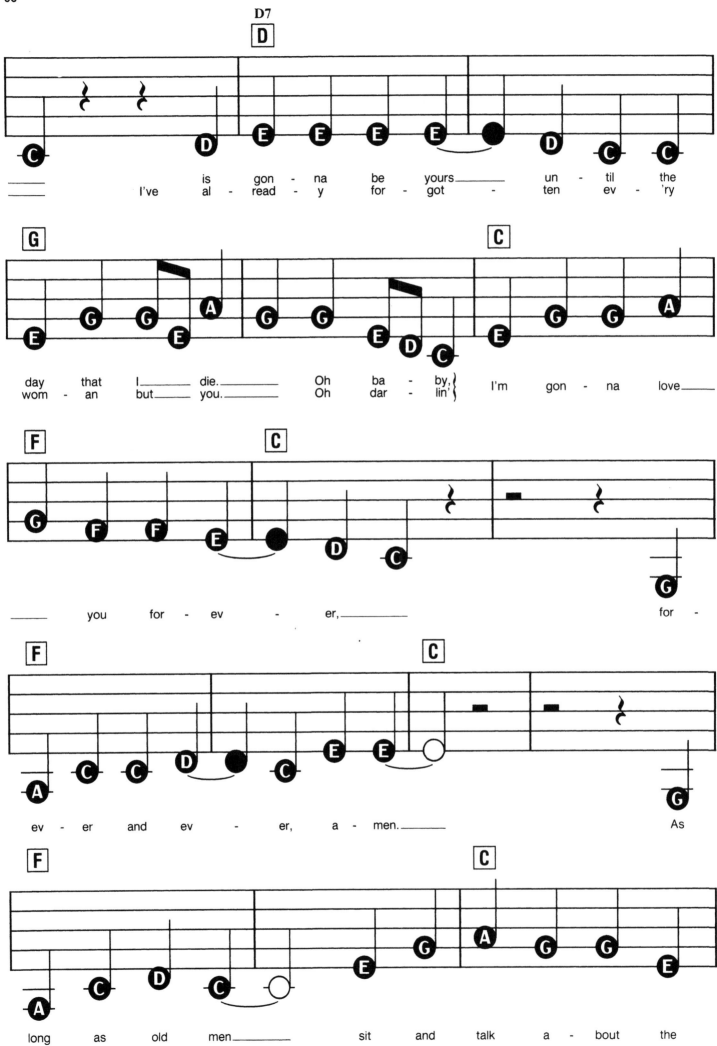

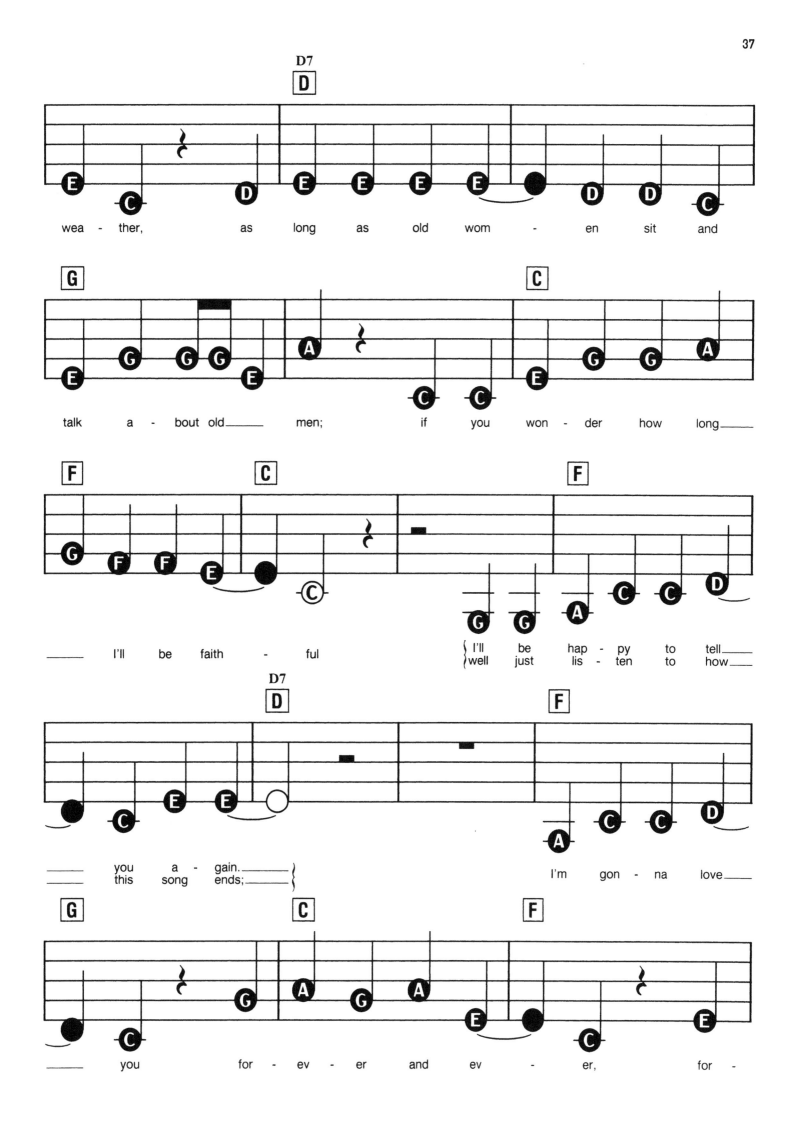

38

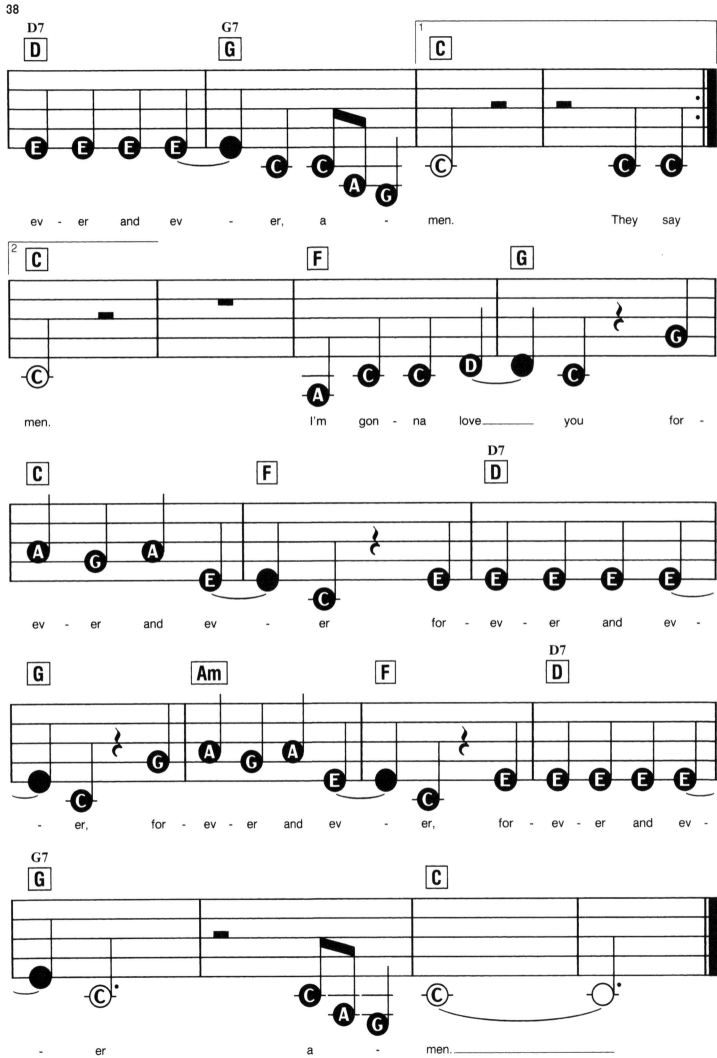

Friends in Low Places

Registration 1
Rhythm: Swing or Country

Words and Music by DeWayne Blackwell
and Earl Bud Lee

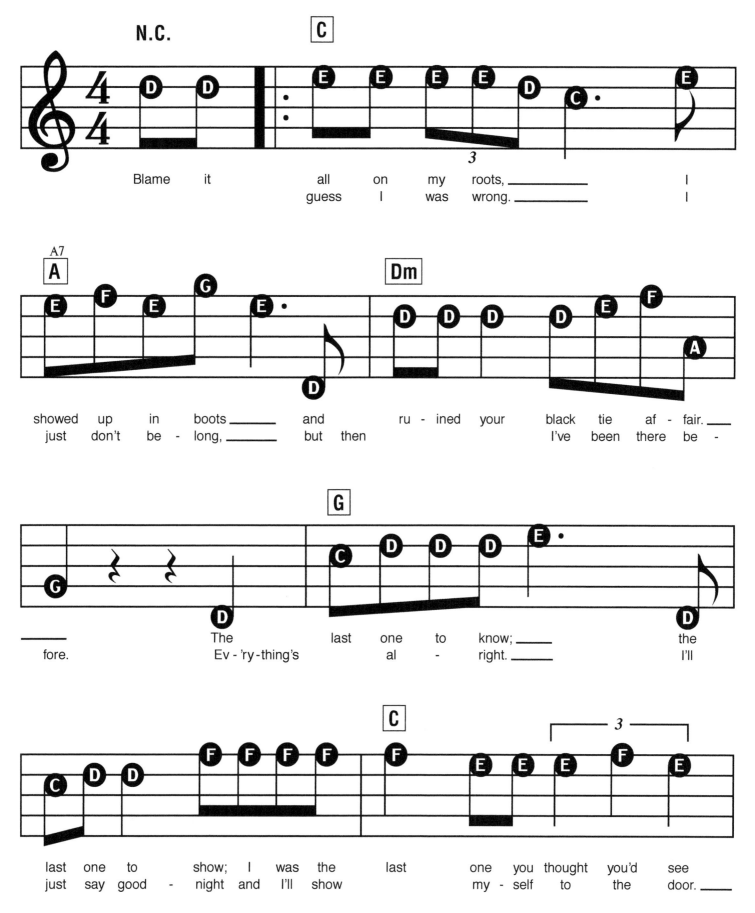

Blame it all on my roots, _____ I
guess I was wrong. _____ I

showed up in boots _____ and ru - ined your black tie af - fair. ____
just don't be - long, _____ but then I've been there be -

fore. Ev - 'ry-thing's al - right. _____ the

last one to know; _____ the
I'll

last one to show; I was the last one you thought you'd see
just say good - night and I'll show my - self to the door. ____

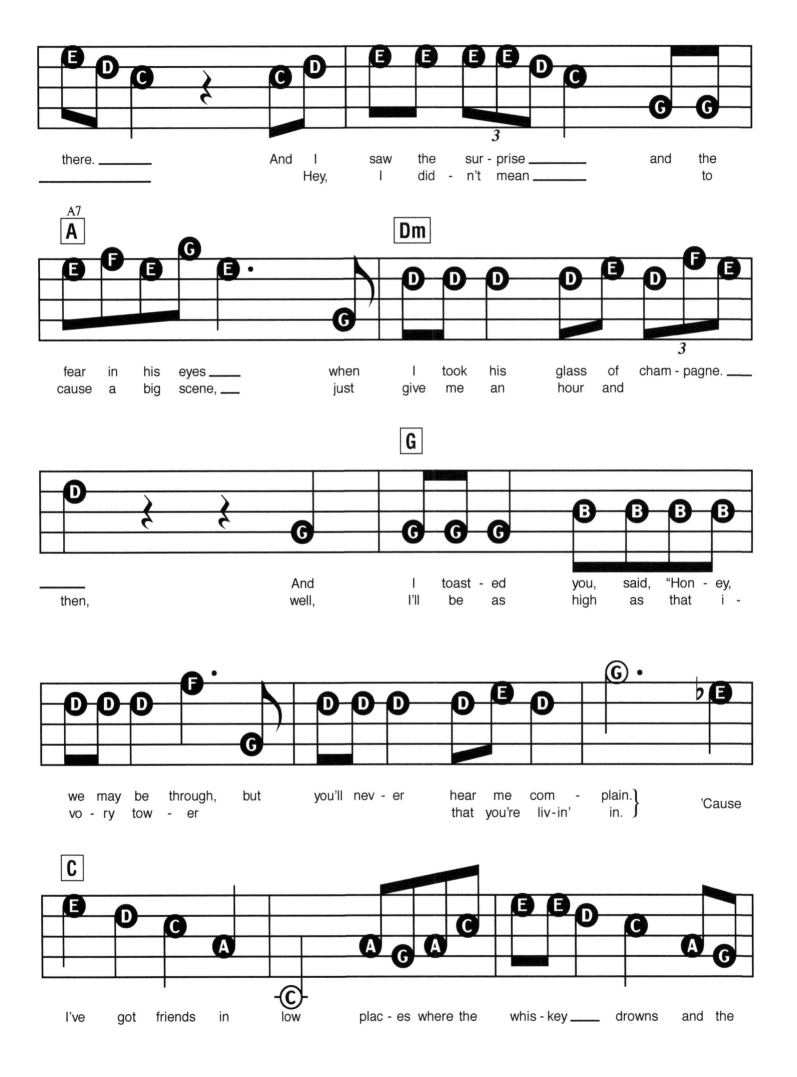

40

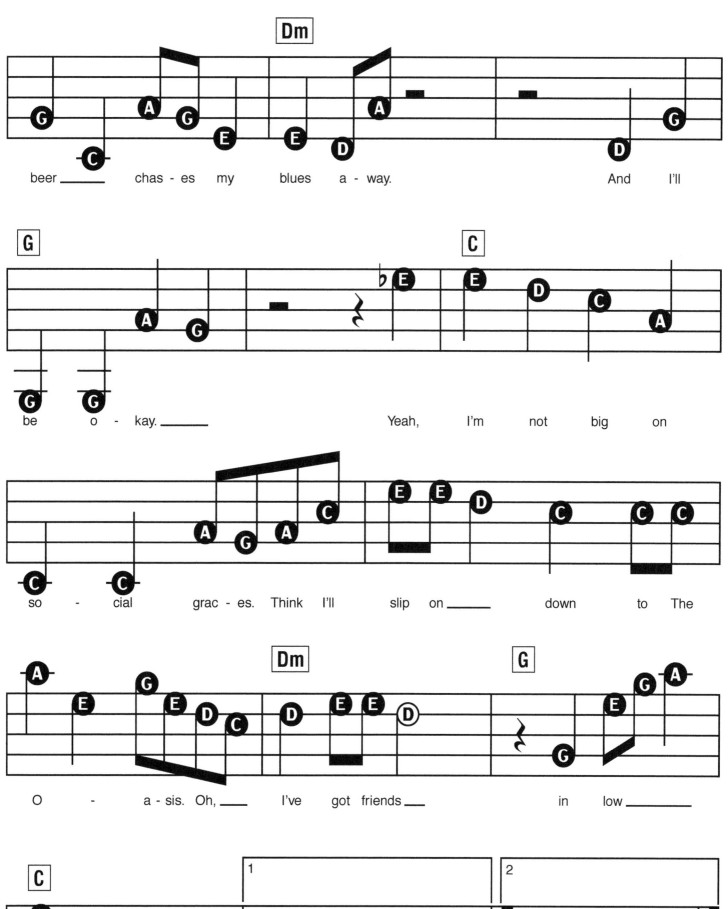

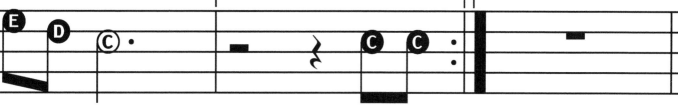

Funny How Time Slips Away

Registration 1
Rhythm: Country

Words and Music by
Willie Nelson

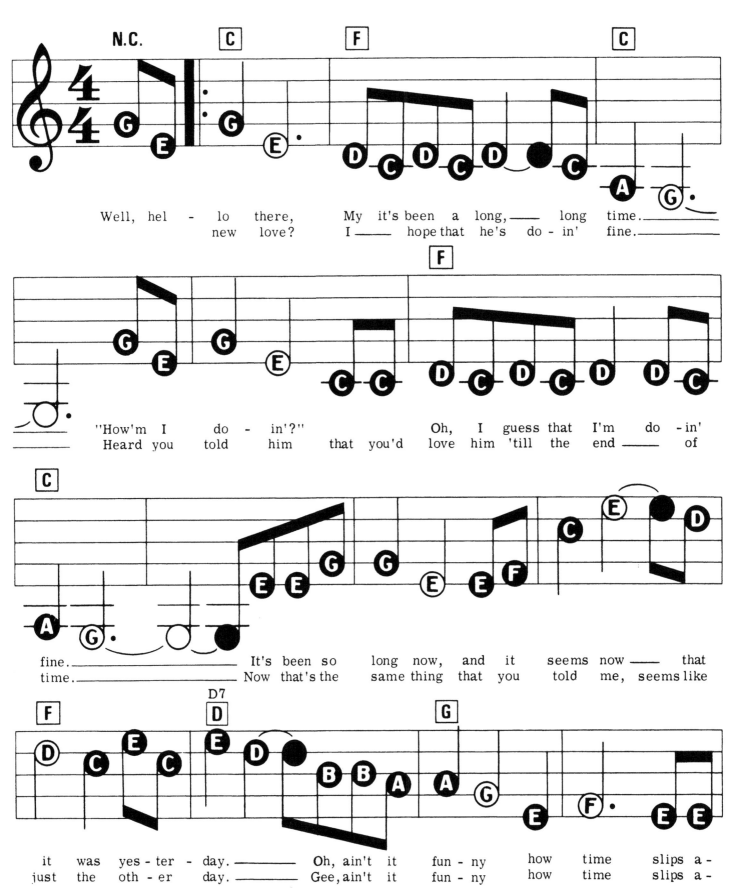

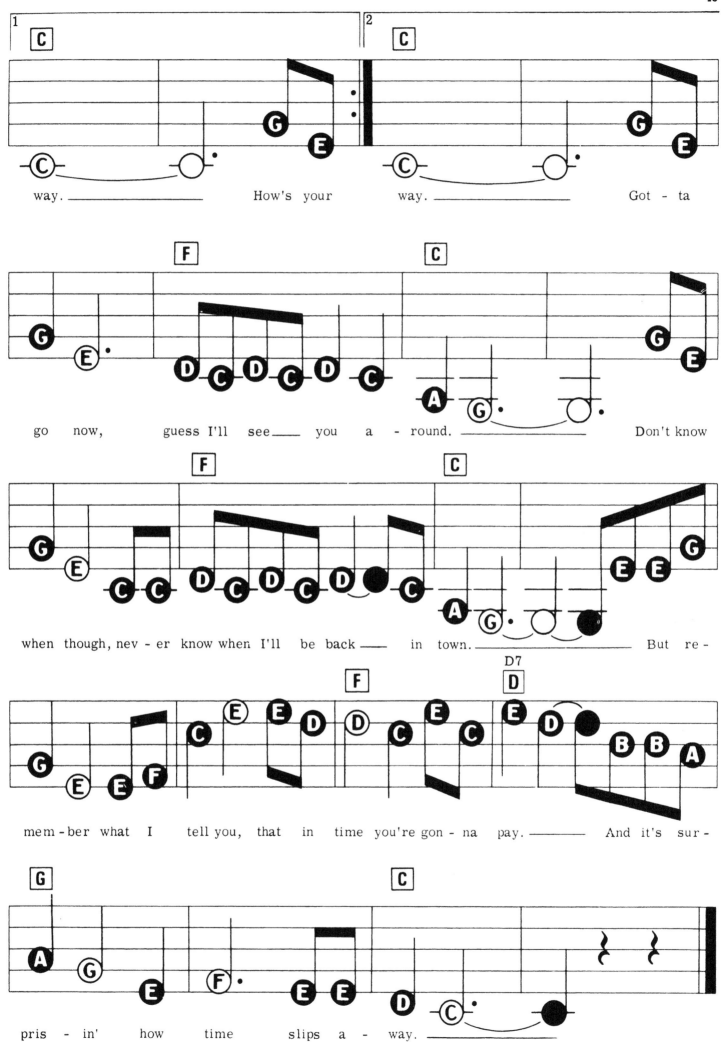

Galveston

Registration 8
Rhythm: Folk Ballad or 4/4 Ballad

Words and Music by
Jimmy Webb

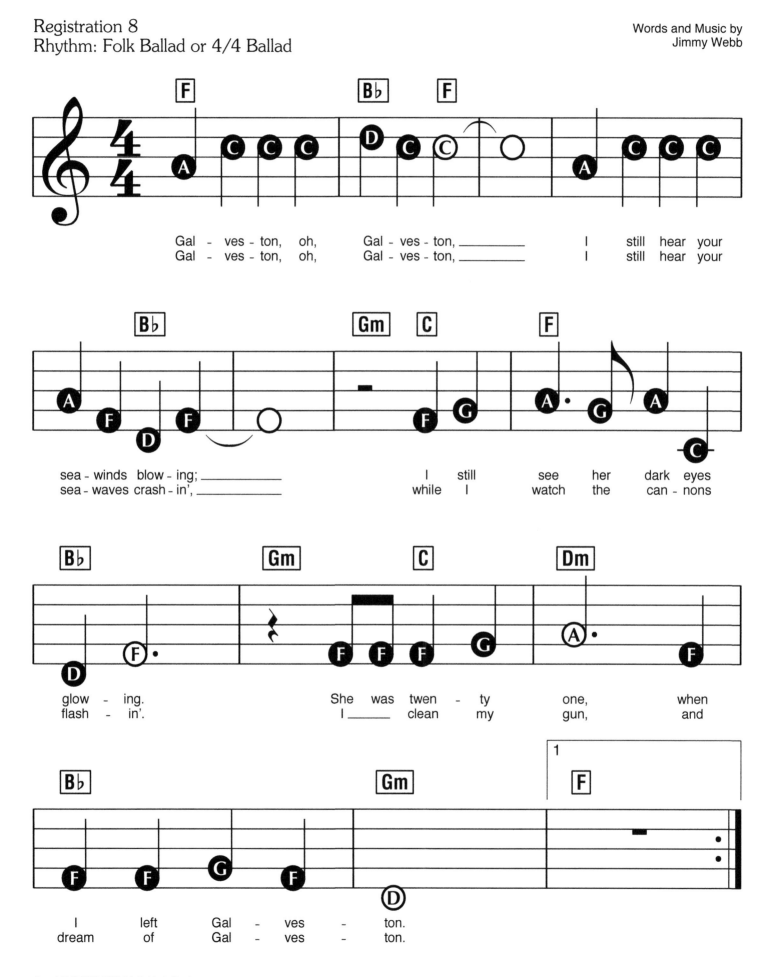

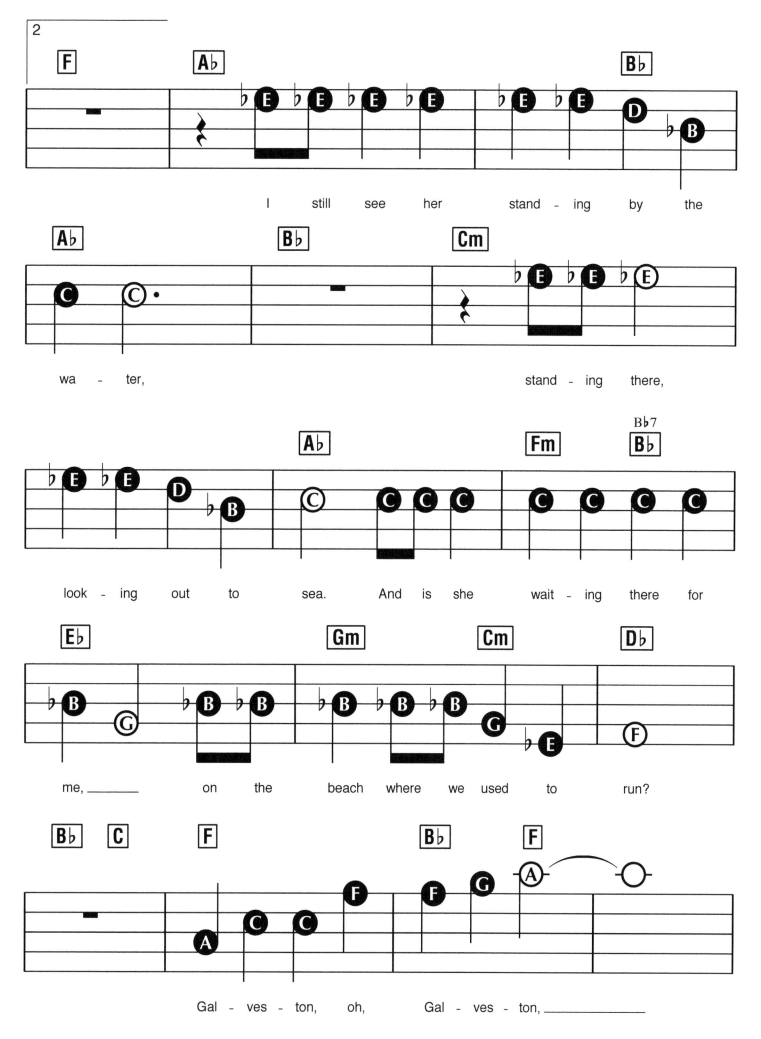

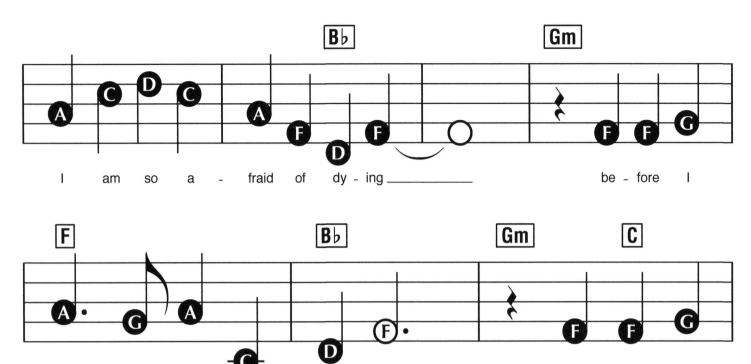

I am so a - fraid of dy - ing _____ be - fore I

dry the tears she's cry - ing, be - fore I

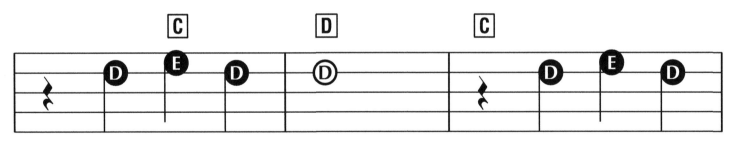

watch your sea birds fly - ing in the sun _____

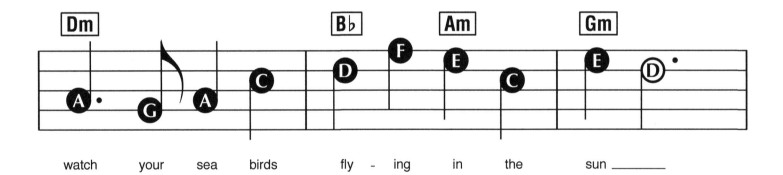

at Gal - ves - ton, at Gal - ves -

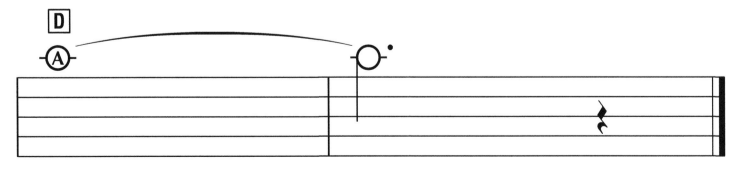

ton. _____

Jolene

Registration 7
Rhythm: Country Pop or 8-Beat

Words and Music by
Dolly Parton

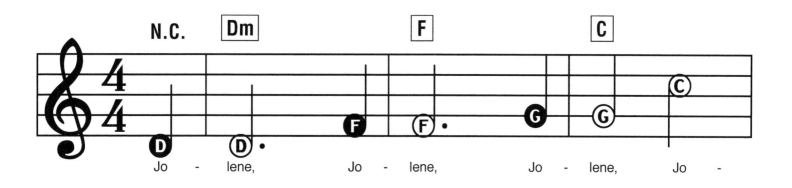

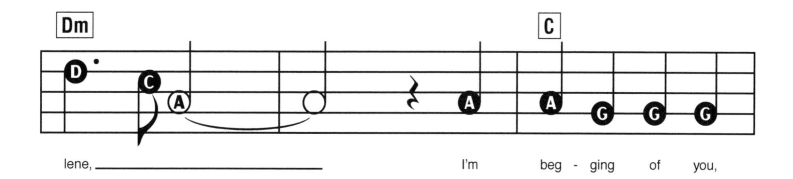

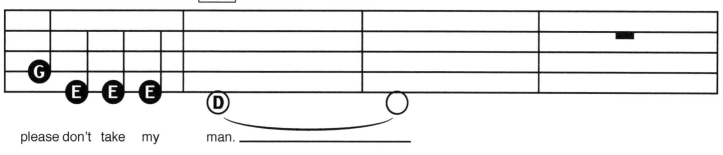

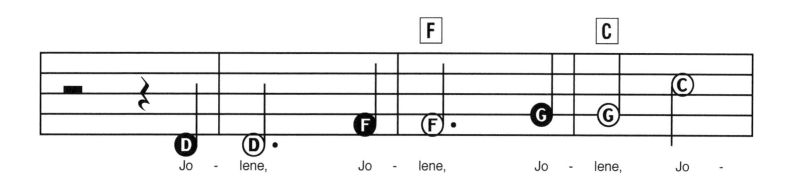

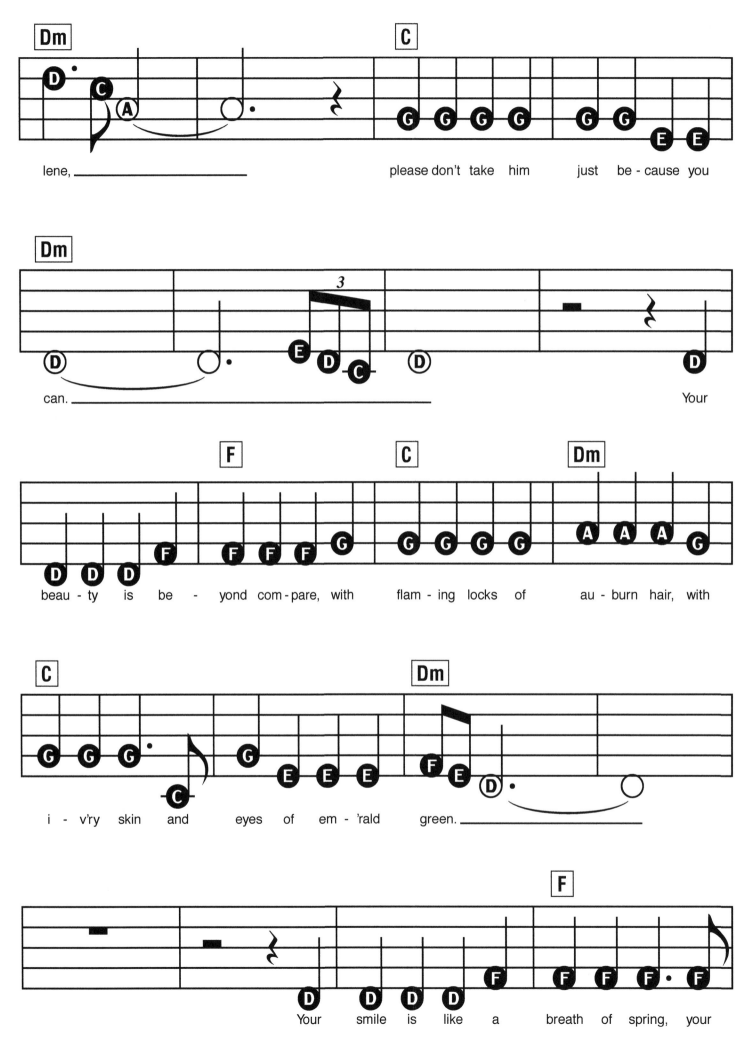

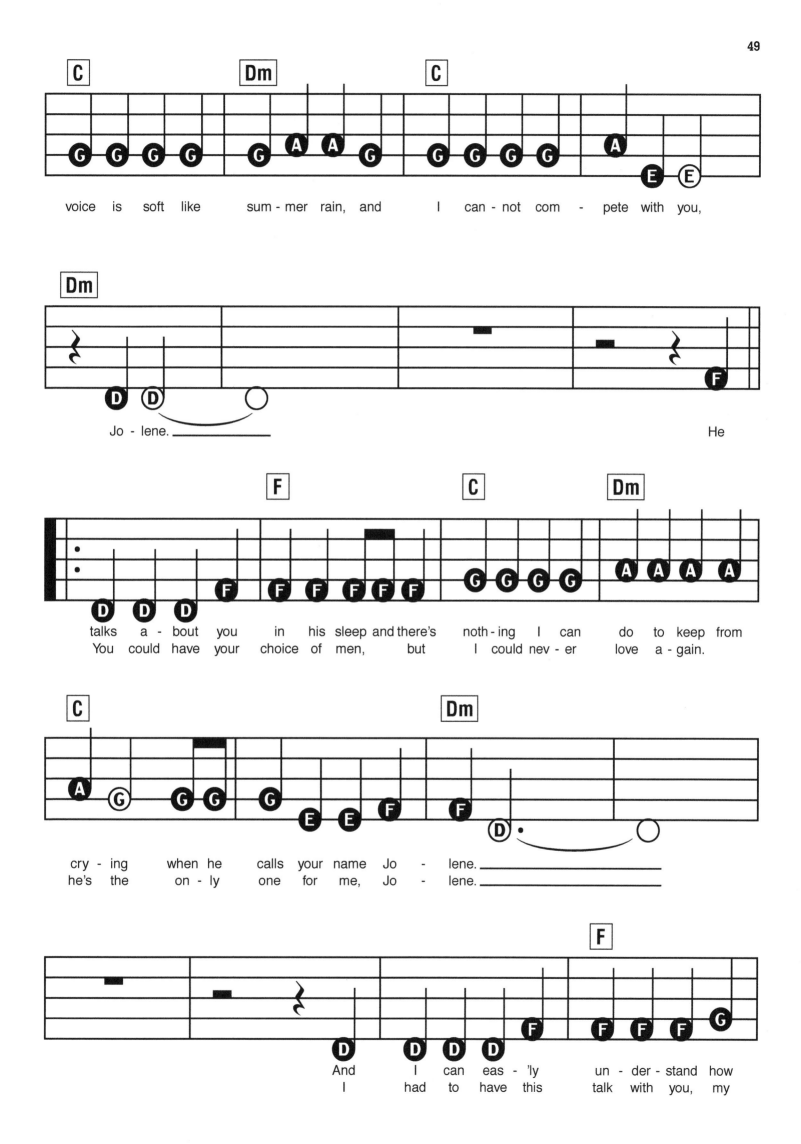

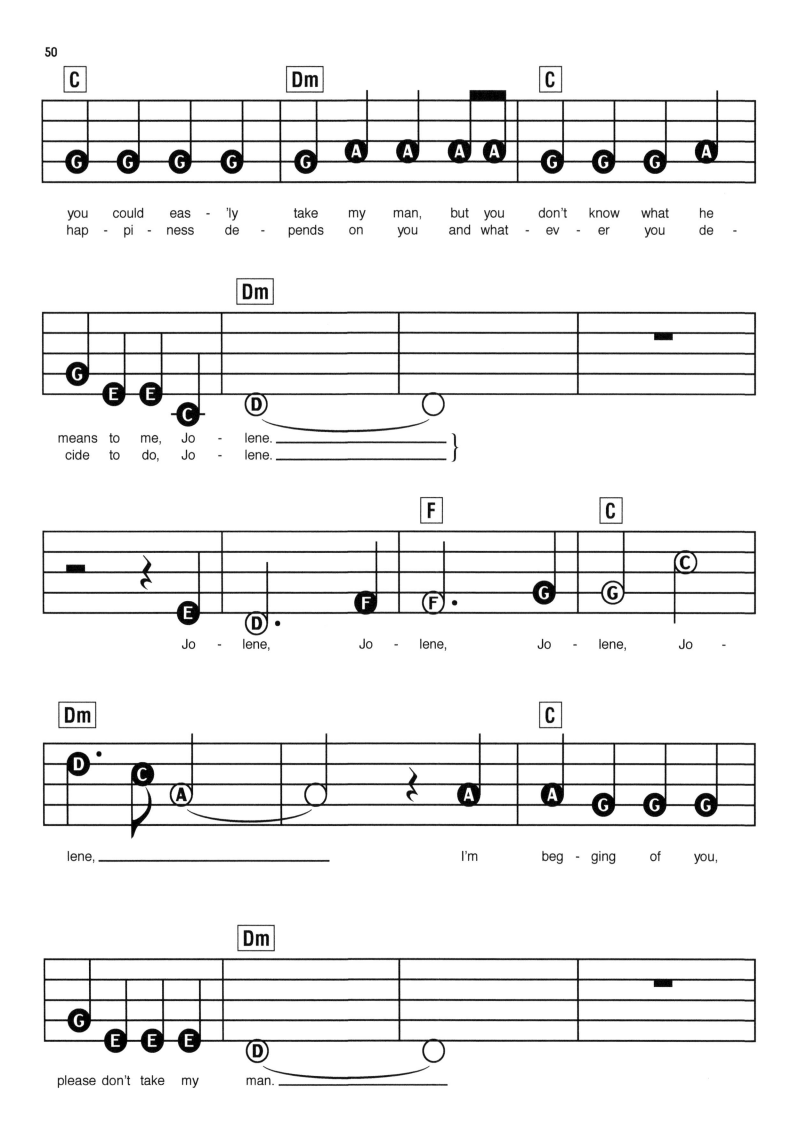

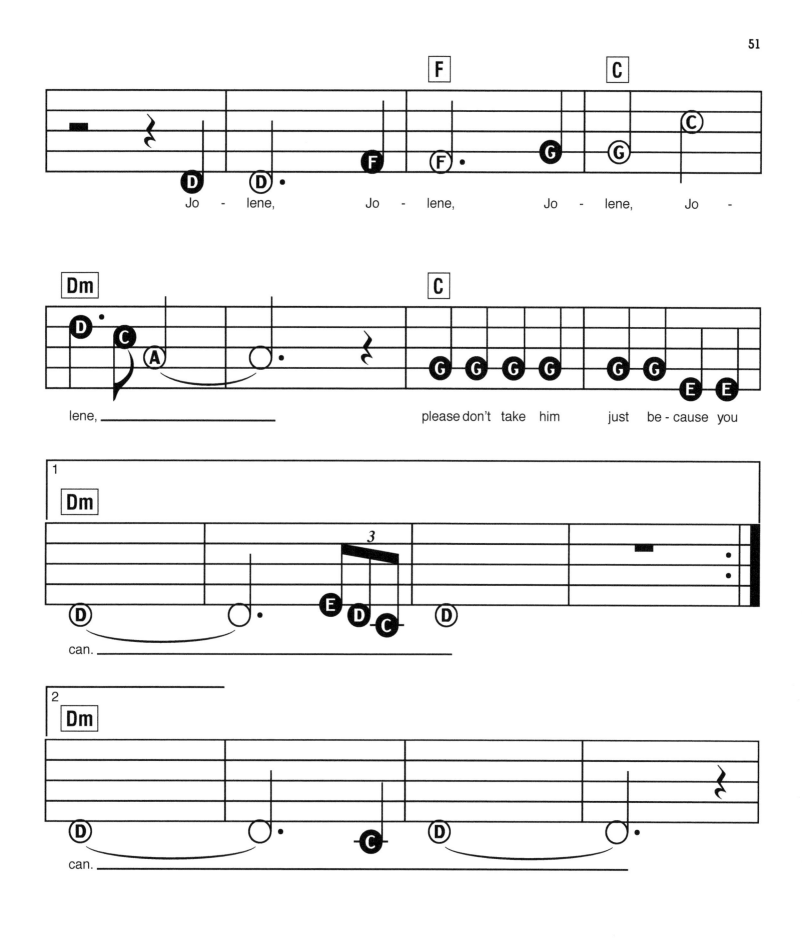

Jo - lene,   Jo - lene,   Jo - lene,   Jo -

lene, _____   please don't take him   just be - cause you

can. _____

can. _____

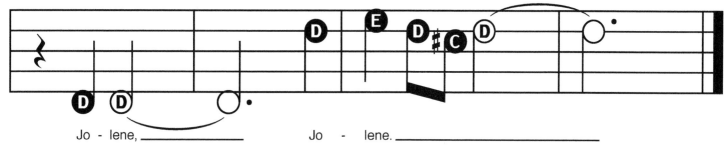

Jo - lene, _____   Jo - lene. _____

Gentle on My Mind

Registration 10
Rhythm: Fox Trot or Pops

Words and Music by
John Hartford

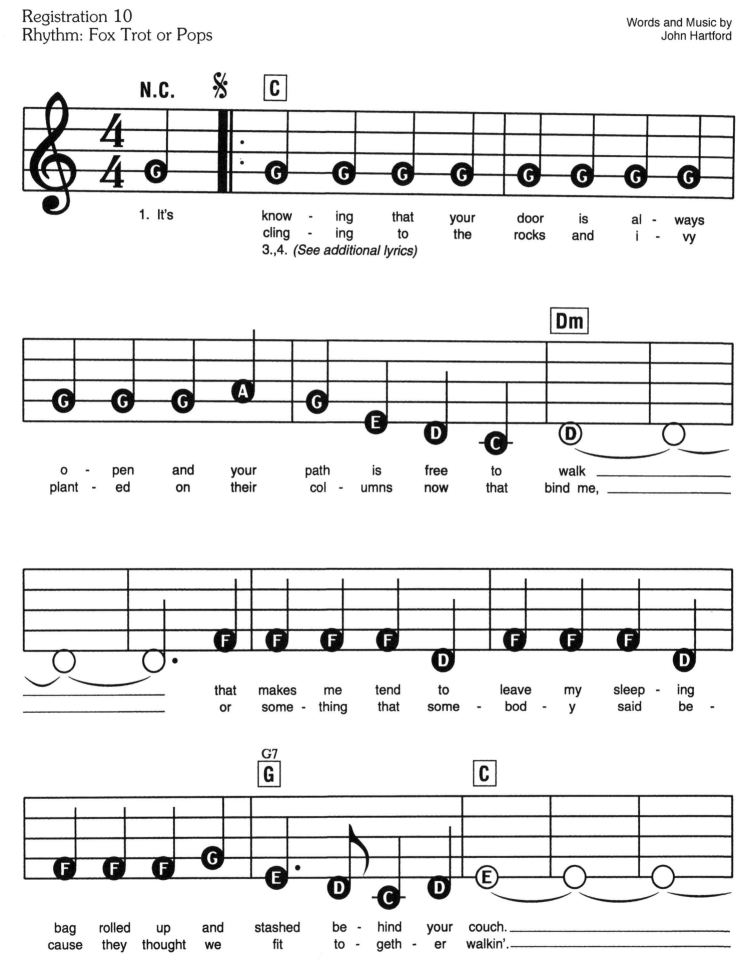

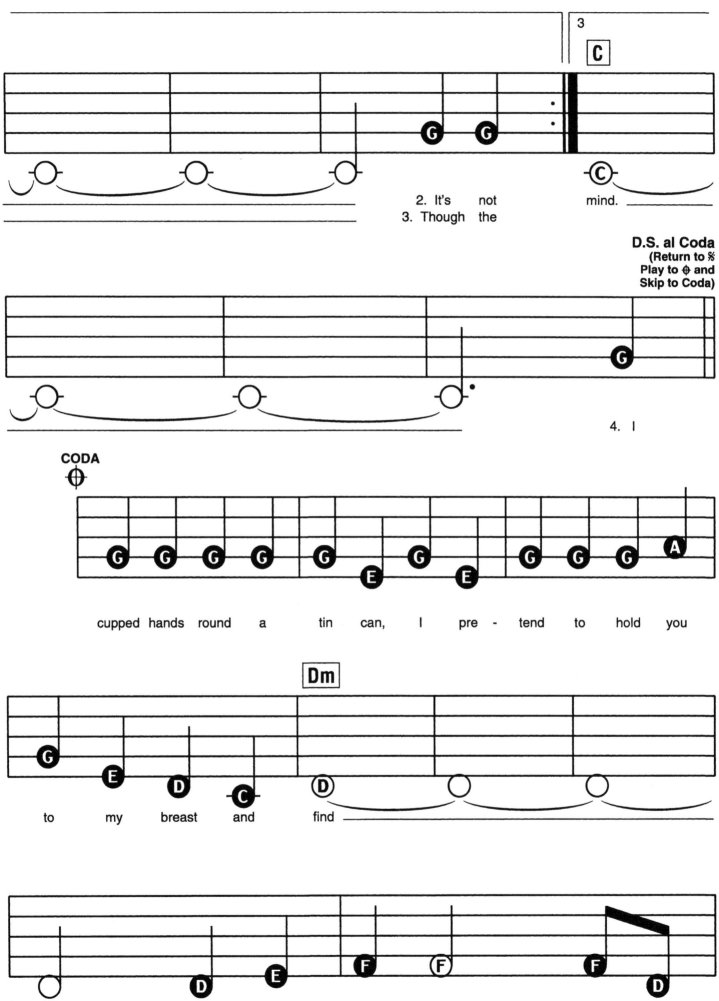

2. It's not
3. Though the

mind.

D.S. al Coda
(Return to %
Play to ⊕ and
Skip to Coda)

4. I

CODA
⊕

cupped hands round a tin can, I pre - tend to hold you

Dm

to my breast and find

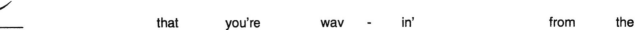

that you're wav - in' from the

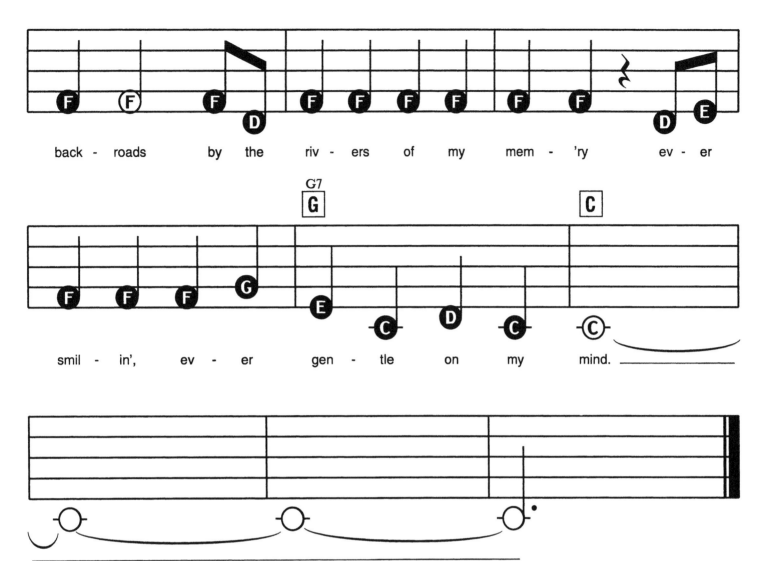

back - roads   by   the   riv - ers   of   my   mem - 'ry   ev - er

smil - in',   ev - er   gen - tle   on   my   mind. _____

Additional Lyrics

3. Though the wheat fields and the clotheslines
   and the junkyards and the highways come between us,
   and some other woman cryin' to her mother
   'cause she turned and I was gone.
   I still might run in silence,
   tears of joy might stain my face,
   and the summer sun might burn me till I'm blind,
   but not to where I cannot see you
   walkin' on the backroads
   by the rivers flowing gentle on my mind.

4. I dip my cup of soup back from some gurglin',
   cracklin' cauldron in some train yard,
   my beard a rough'ning coal pile and
   a dirty hat pulled low across my face.
   Through cupped hands round a tin can,
   I pretend to hold you to my breast and find
   that you're wavin' from the backroads
   by the rivers of my mem'ry,
   ever smilin', ever gentle on my mind.

Green Green Grass of Home

Registration 2
Rhythm: Country

Words and Music by
Curly Putman

N.C. | **C** | **F**

The old home-town looks the same as I step down from the
old house ___ is still stand-ing, though the paint is cracked and

C

train, _____ and there to greet me is my ma - ma ___ and
dry, _____ and there's that old oak tree ___ that I used ___ to

G7
G | **C**

pa - pa. Down the road I look and
play on. Down the road I walk with

C7
F

there runs Mar - y, } hair of gold and lips like cher - ries. It's
my sweet Mar - y, }

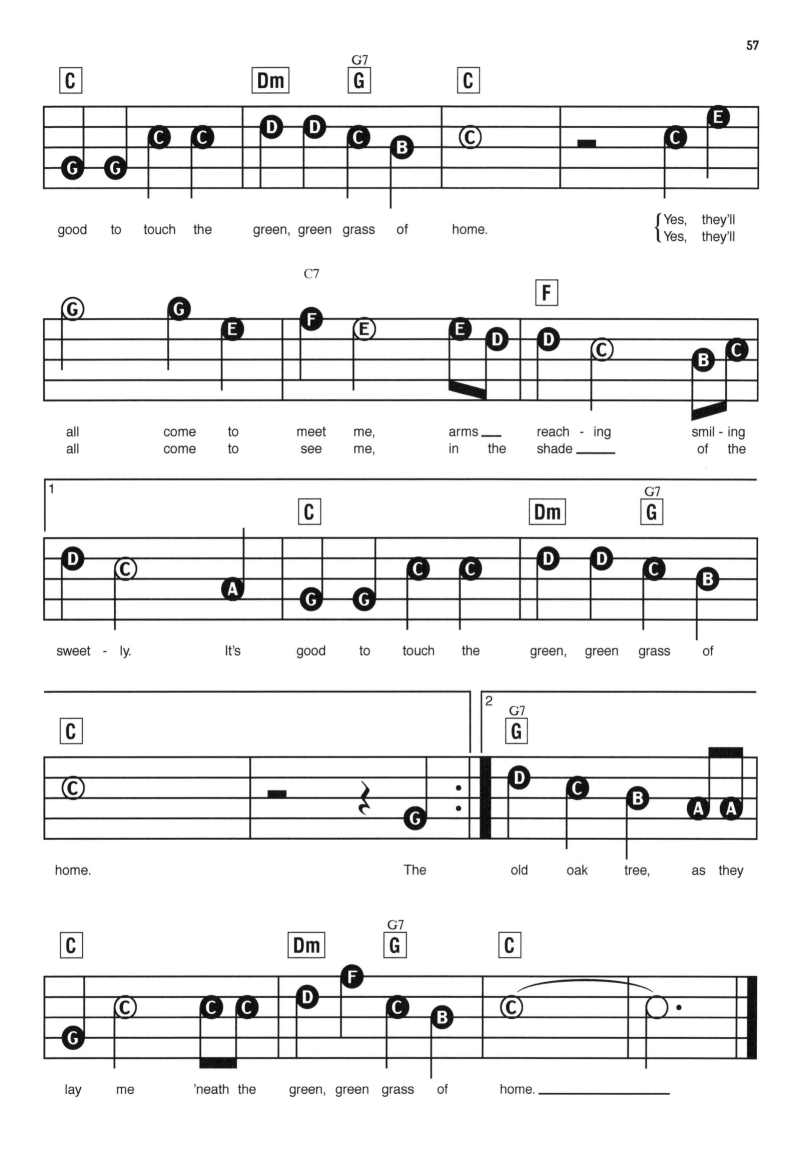

Have I Told You Lately That I Love You

Registration 8
Rhythm: Country Western or Fox Trot

Words and Music by
Scott Wiseman

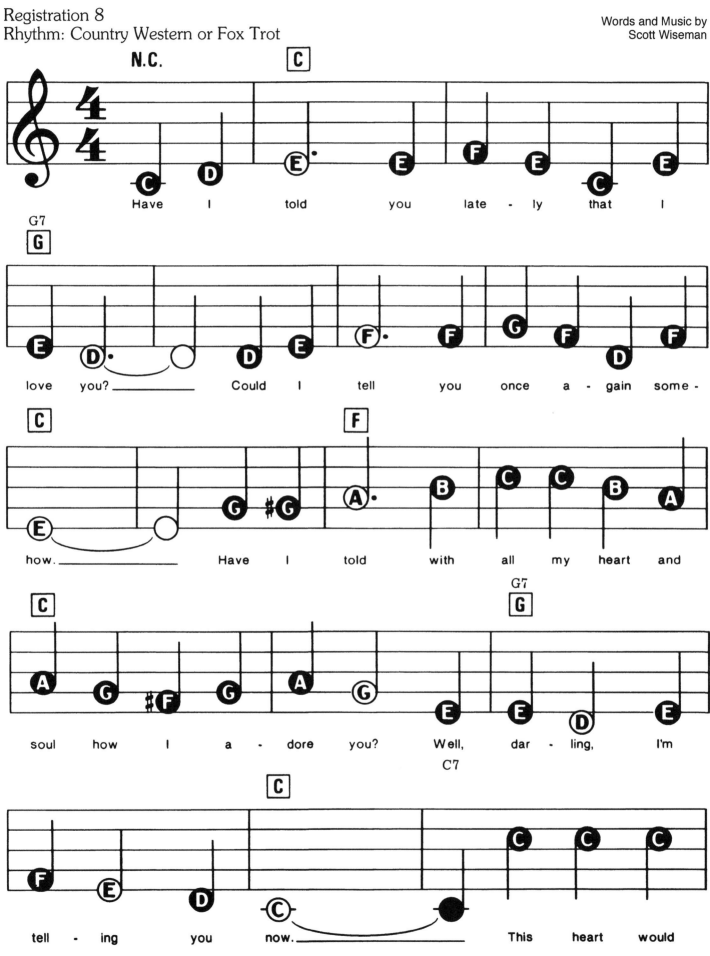

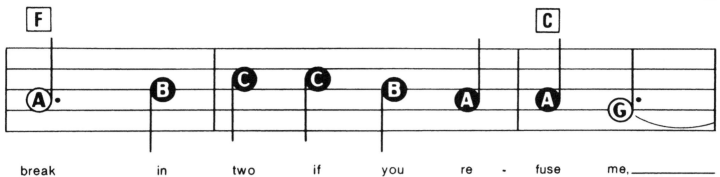

break   in   two   if   you   re -   fuse   me, _____

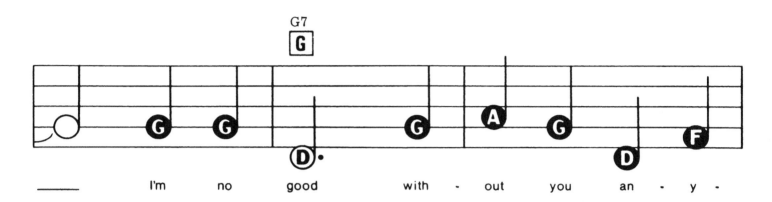

_____   I'm   no   good   with - out   you   an - y -

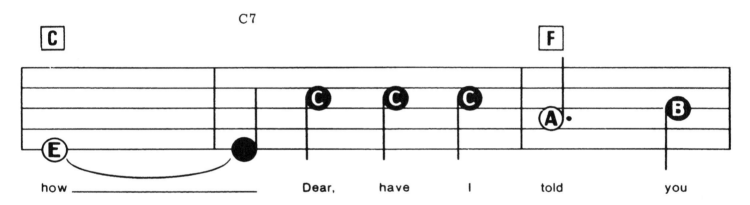

how _____   Dear,   have   I   told   you

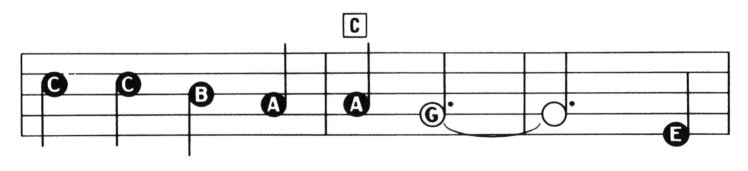

late - ly   that   I   love   you? _____   Well,

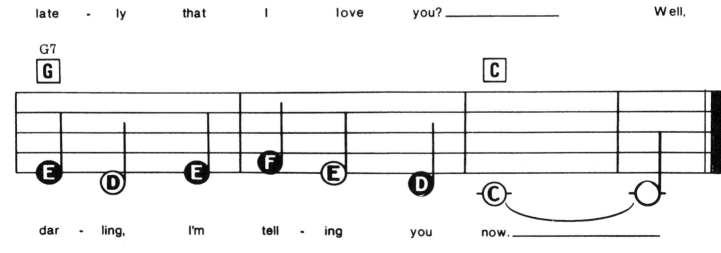

dar - ling,   I'm   tell - ing   you   now. _____

He Stopped Loving Her Today

Registration 8
Rhythm: Country Western or Fox Trot

Words and Music by Bobby Braddock
and Curly Putman

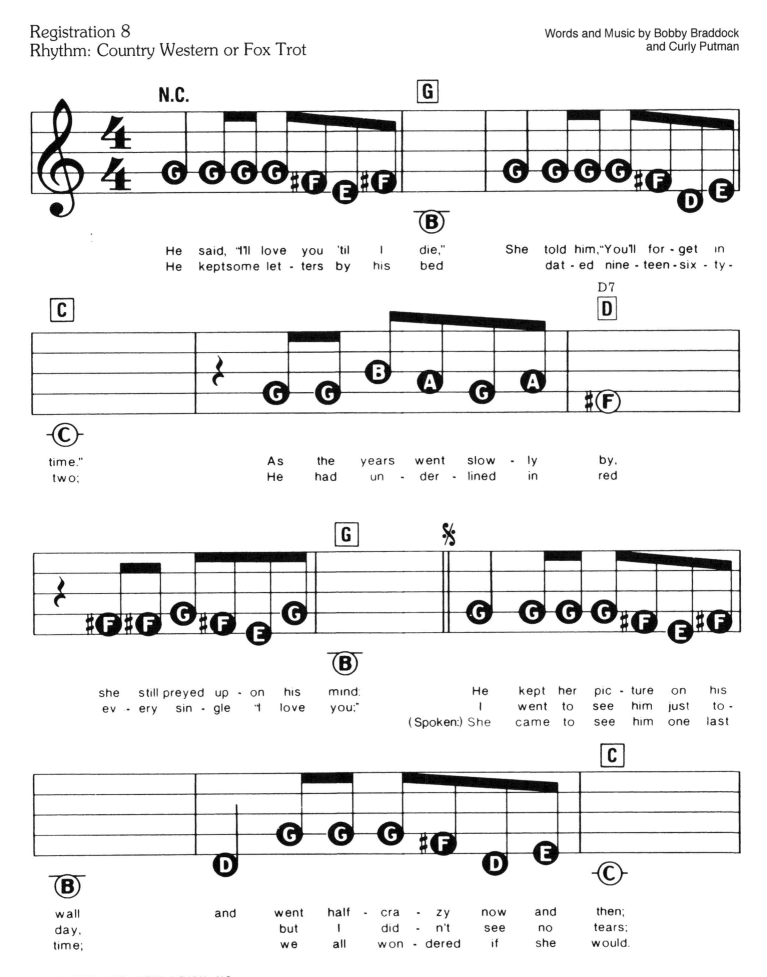

He said, "I'll love you 'til I die," She told him, "You'll for-get in
He kept some let-ters by his bed dat-ed nine-teen-six-ty-

time." As the years went slow-ly by,
two; He had un-der-lined in red

she still preyed up-on his mind: He kept her pic-ture on his
ev-ery sin-gle "I love you;" I went to see him just to-
(Spoken:) She came to see him one last

wall and went half-cra-zy now and then;
day, but I did-n't see no tears;
time; we all won-dered if she would.

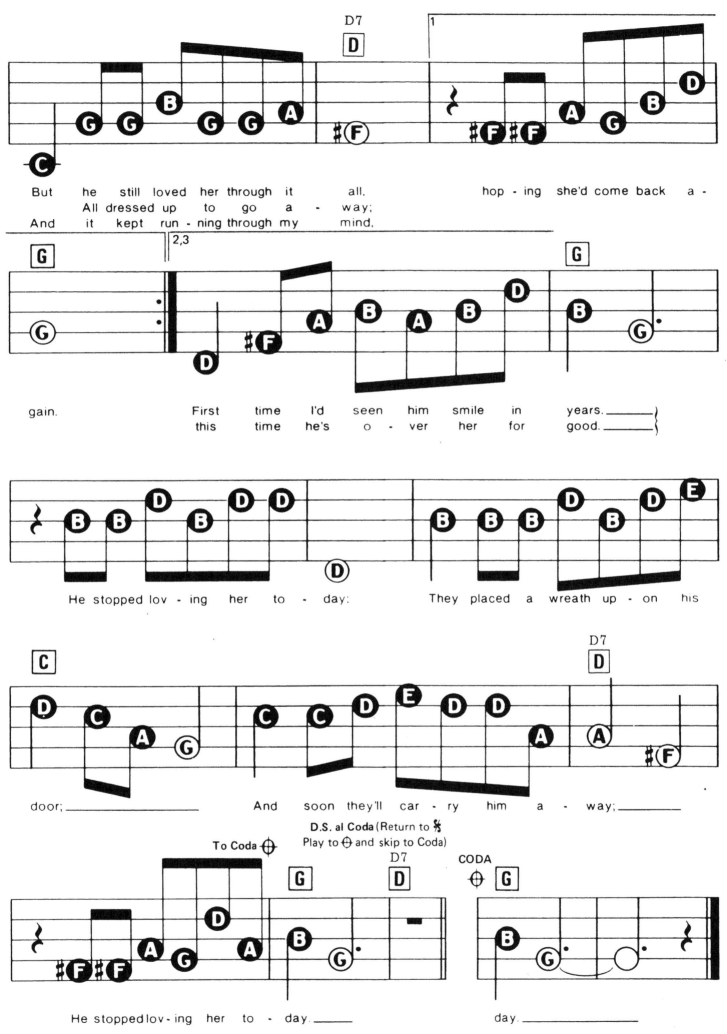

But he still loved her through it all, hop - ing she'd come back a -
All dressed up to go a - way;
And it kept run - ning through my mind,

gain.
this time he's o - ver her for good. ____}
First time I'd seen him smile in years. ____}

He stopped lov - ing her to - day;
They placed a wreath up - on his

door; ____
And soon they'll car - ry him a - way; ____

To Coda

D.S. al Coda (Return to %
Play to and skip to Coda)

CODA

He stopped lov - ing her to - day. ____

day. ____

Heartaches by the Number

Registration 4
Rhythm: Country

Words and Music by
Harlan Howard

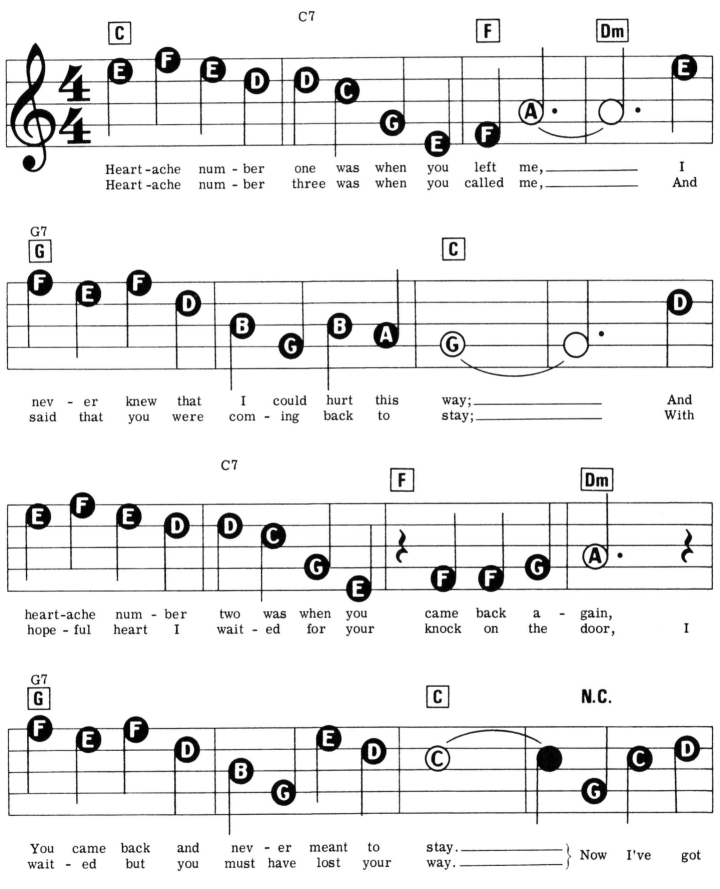

Heart - ache num - ber one was when you left me, _____ I
Heart - ache num - ber three was when you called me, _____ And

nev - er knew that I could hurt this way; _____ And
said that you were com - ing back to stay; _____ With

heart - ache num - ber two was when you came back a - gain, I
hope - ful heart I wait - ed for your knock on the door, I

You came back and nev - er meant to stay. _____ } Now I've got
wait - ed but you must have lost your way. _____ } Now I've got

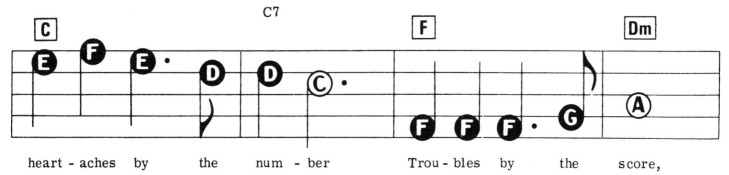

heart - aches   by   the   num - ber   Trou - bles   by   the   score,

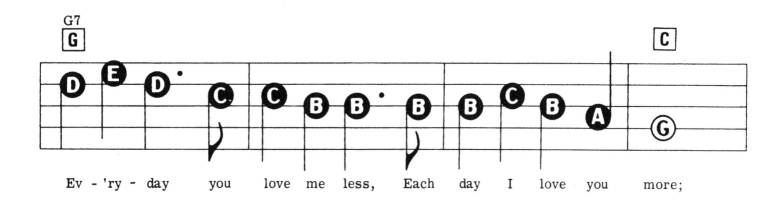

Ev - 'ry - day   you   love me less,   Each   day   I   love you   more;

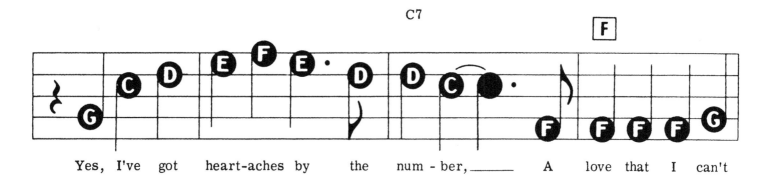

Yes, I've got   heart-aches by   the   num - ber,_____   A   love that I can't

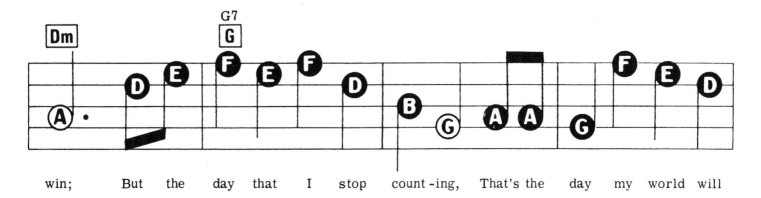

win;   But   the   day   that   I   stop   count-ing, That's the day my world will

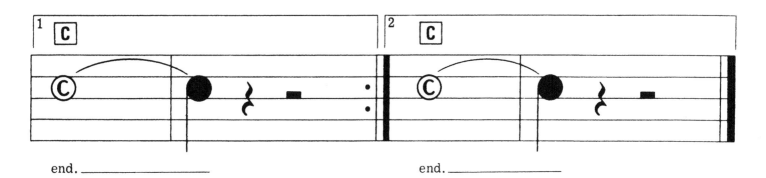

end._____   end._____

Help Me Make It Through the Night

Registration 2
Rhythm: Country

Words and Music by
Kris Kristofferson

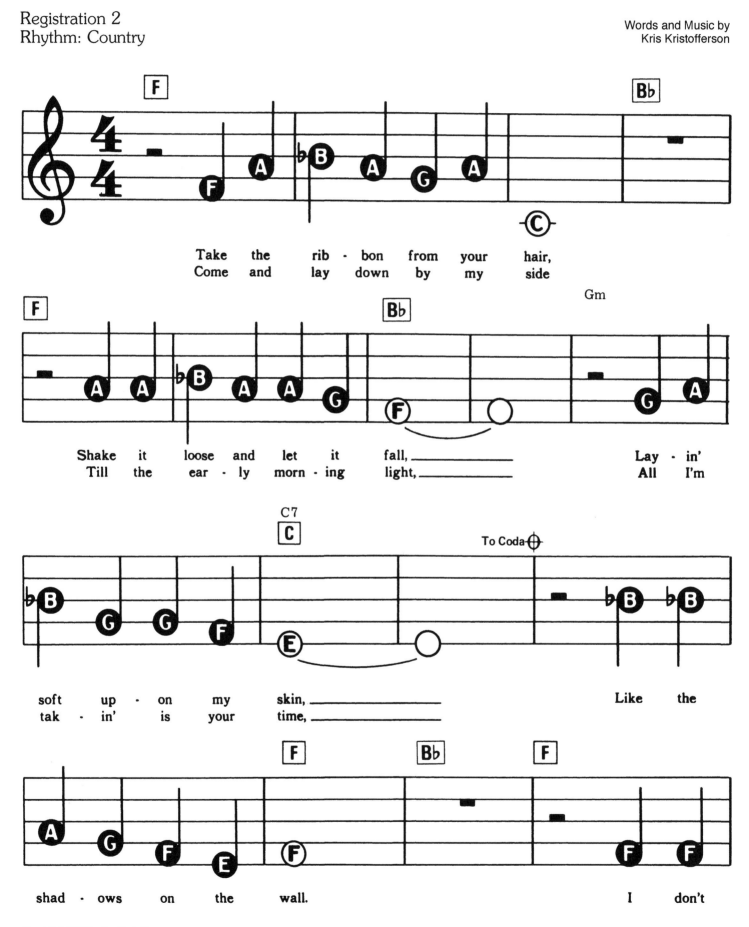

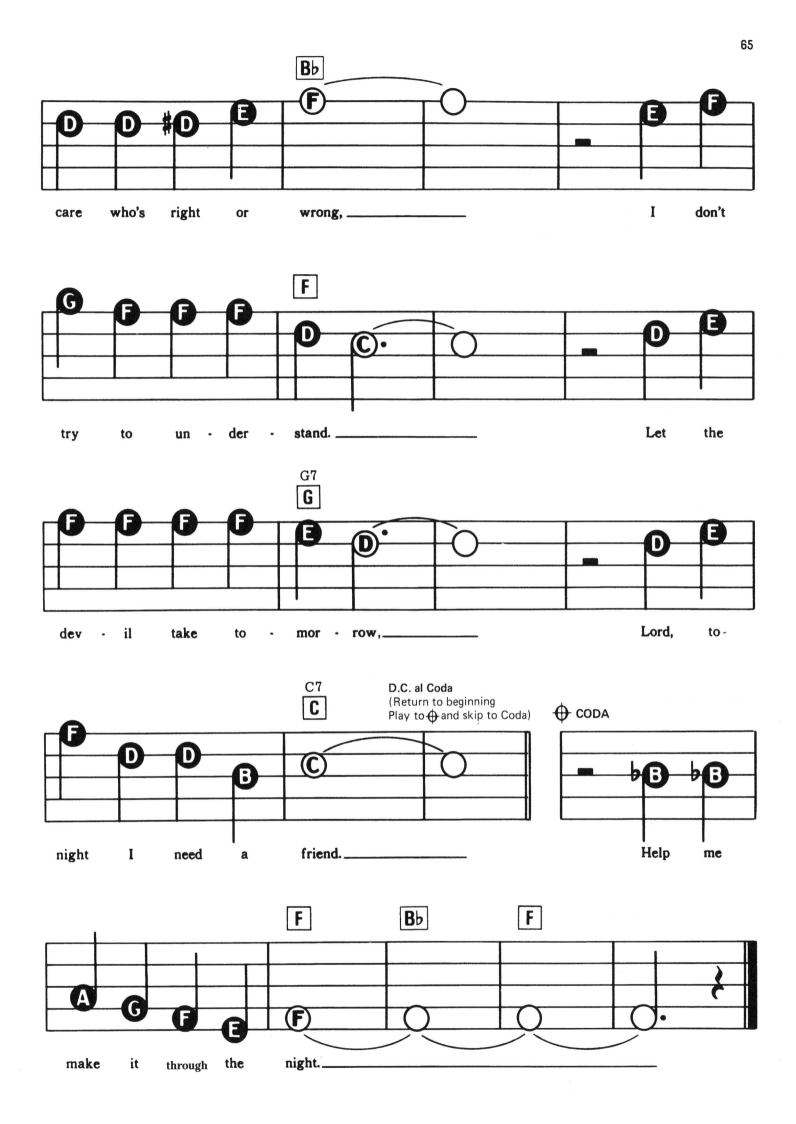

Hey, Good Lookin'

Registration 7
Rhythm: Country Swing or Fox Trot

Words and Music by
Hank Williams

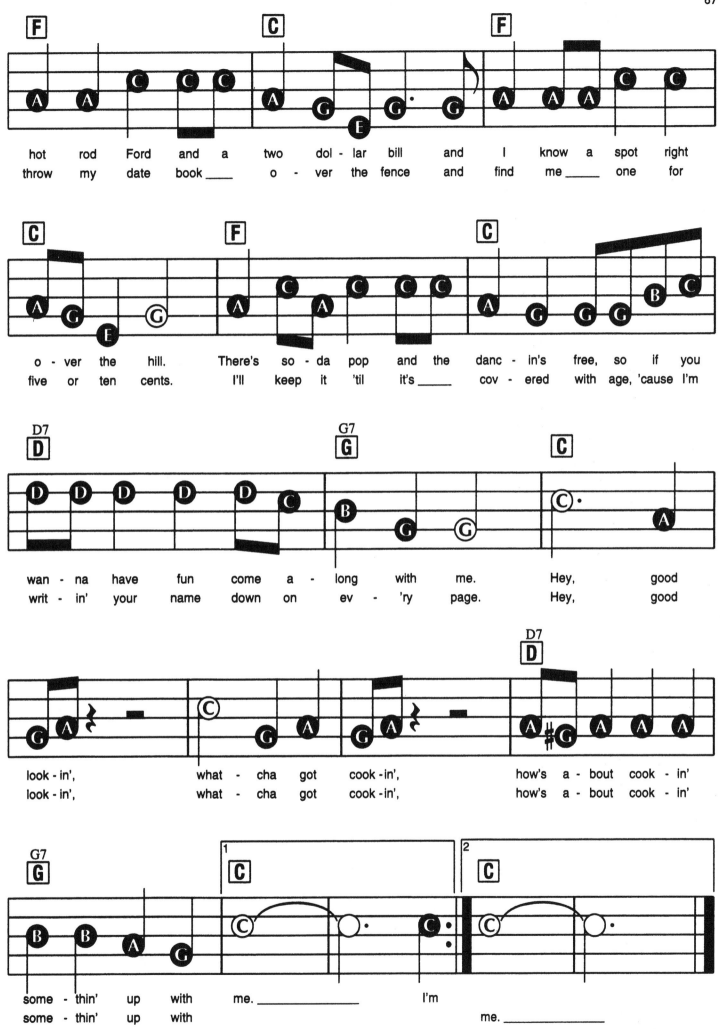

I Can't Stop Loving You

Registration 8
Rhythm: Swing or Fox Trot

Words and Music by
Don Gibson

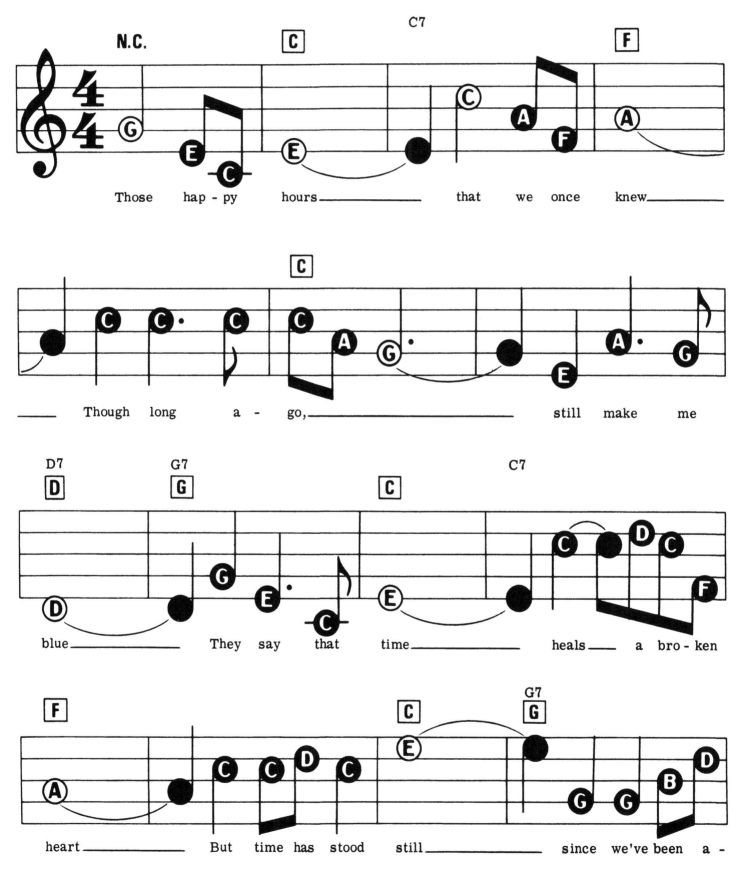

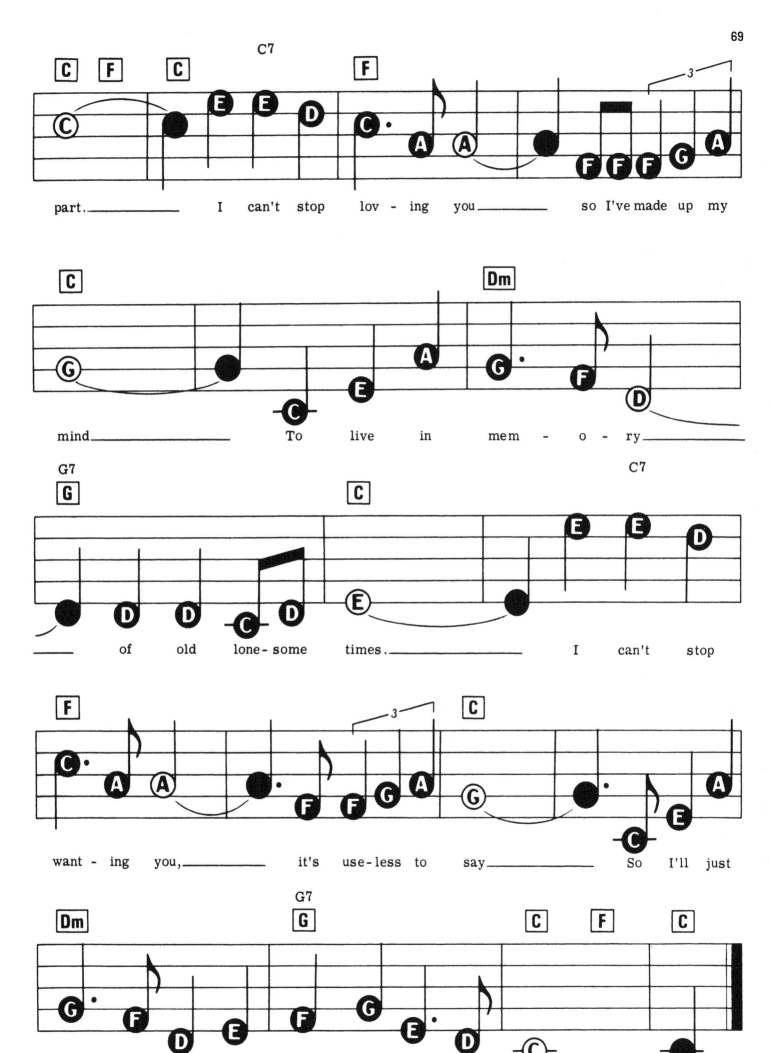

I Fall to Pieces

Registration 9
Rhythm: Country or Shuffle

Words and Music by Hank Cochran
and Harlan Howard

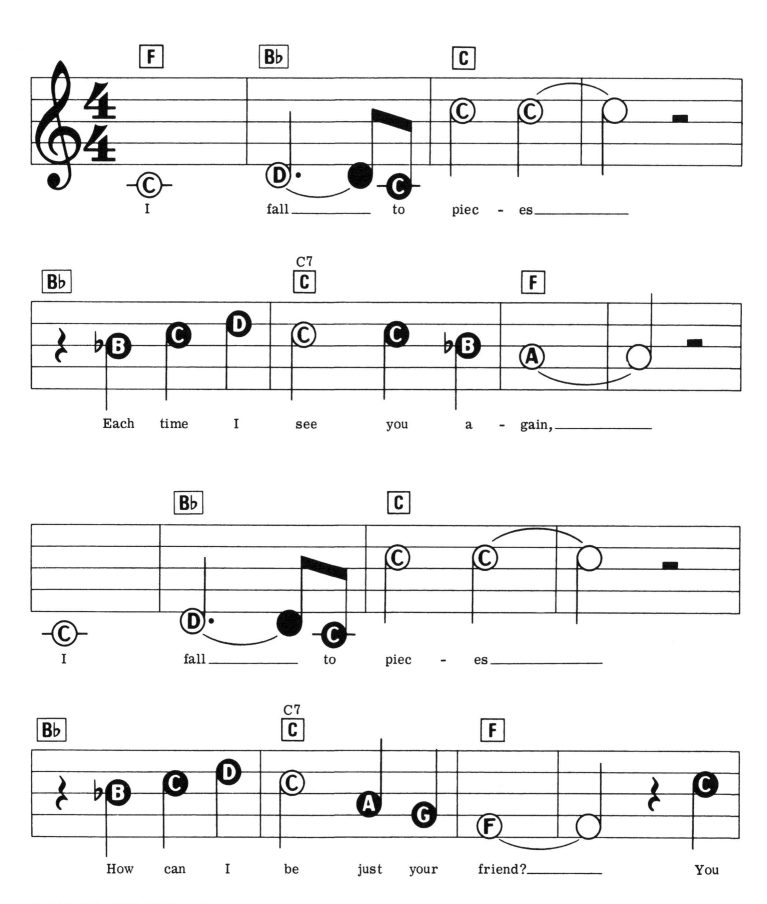

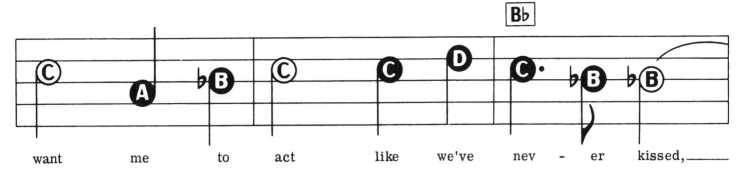

want me to act like we've nev - er kissed,_____

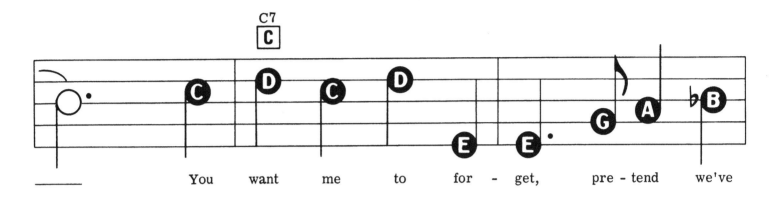

_____ You want me to for - get, pre - tend we've

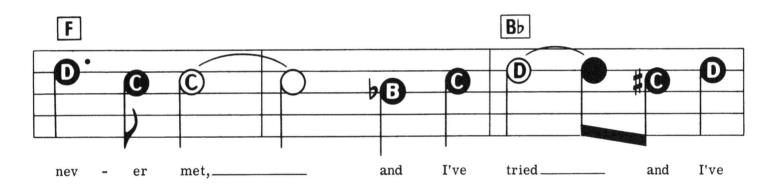

nev - er met,_____ and I've tried____ and I've

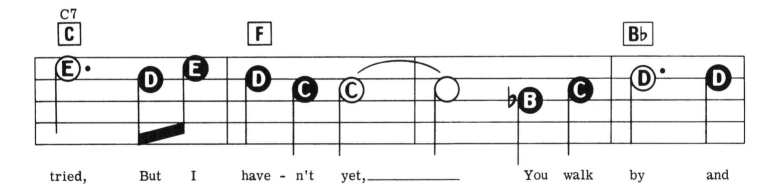

tried, But I have-n't yet,_____ You walk by and

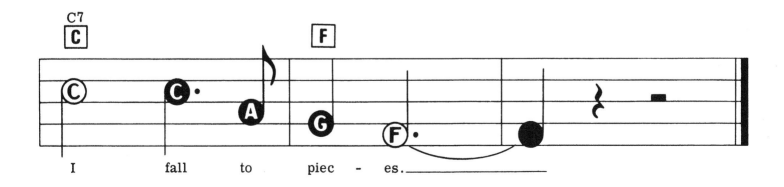

I fall to piec - es._____

I Walk the Line

Registration 8
Rhythm: Country or Ballad

Words and Music by
John R. Cash

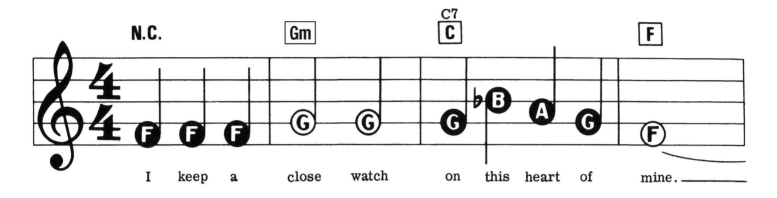

I keep a close watch on this heart of mine.

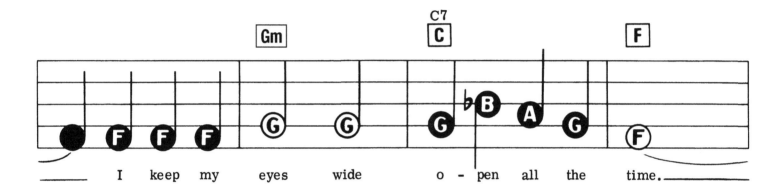

I keep my eyes wide o - pen all the time.

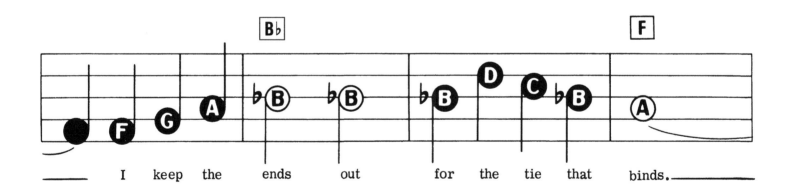

I keep the ends out for the tie that binds.

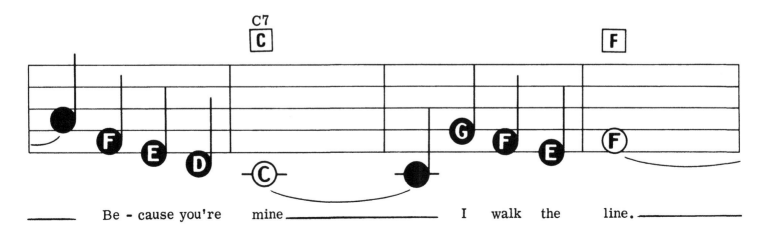

Be - cause you're mine   I walk the line.

73

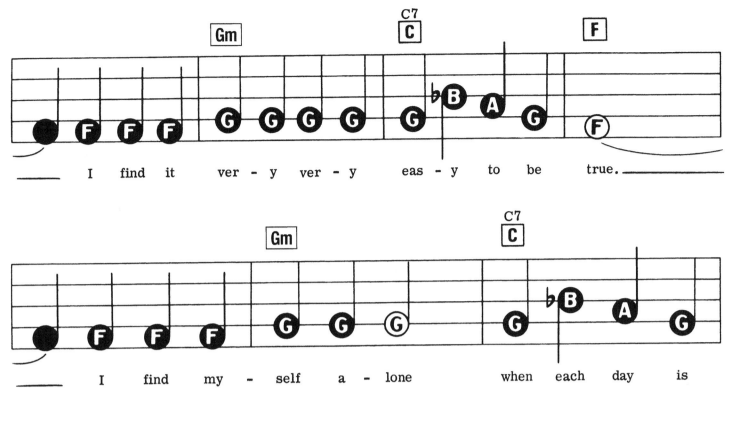

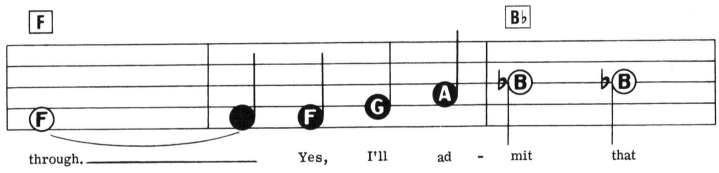

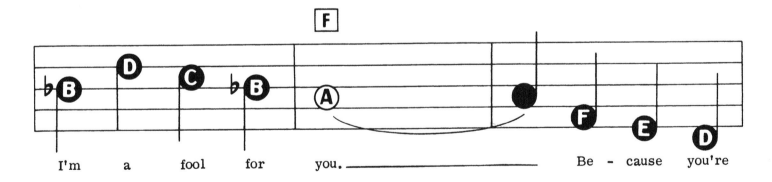

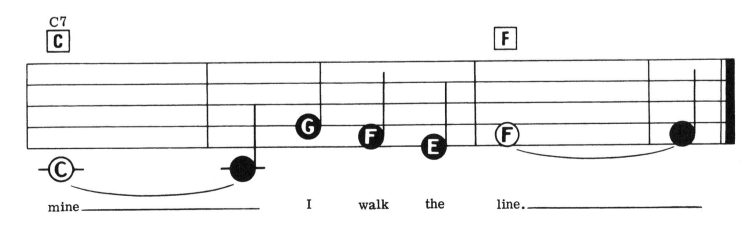

Jambalaya
(On the Bayou)

Registration 4
Rhythm: Fox Trot

Words and Music by
Hank Williams

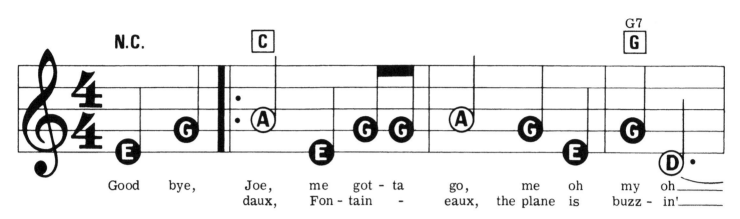

Good bye, Joe, me got - ta go, me oh my oh____
daux, Fon - tain - eaux, the plane is buzz - in'____

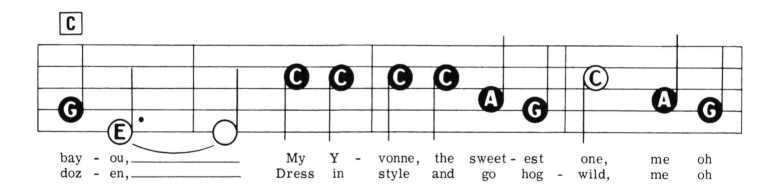

Me got - ta go pole the pi - rogue down the
Kin - folk____ come to see Y - vonne by the

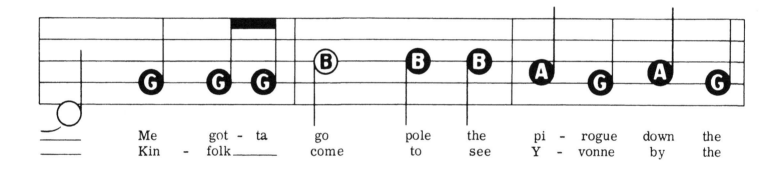

bay - ou,____ My Y - vonne, the sweet - est one, me oh
doz - en,____ Dress in style and go hog - wild, me oh

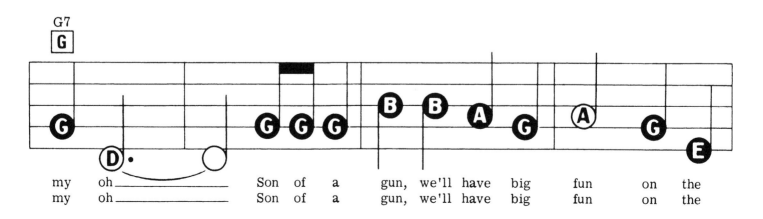

my oh____ Son of a gun, we'll have big fun on the
my oh____ Son of a gun, we'll have big fun on the

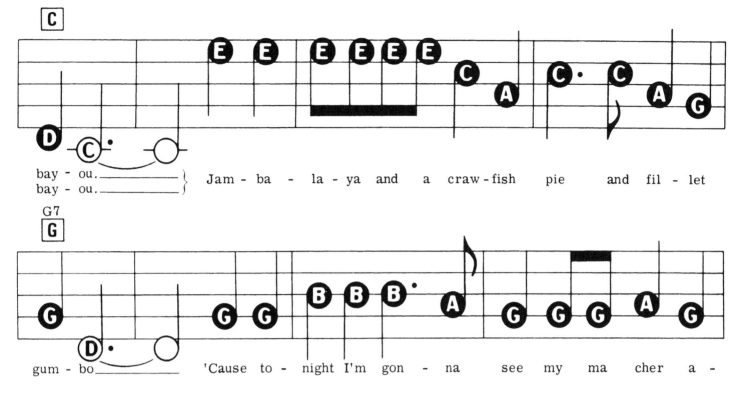

bay - ou._____ } Jam - ba - la - ya and a craw - fish pie and fil - let
bay - ou._____

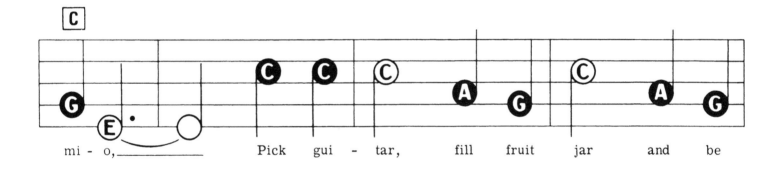

gum - bo_____ 'Cause to - night I'm gon - na see my ma cher a -

Pick gui - tar, fill fruit jar and be

mi - o,_____

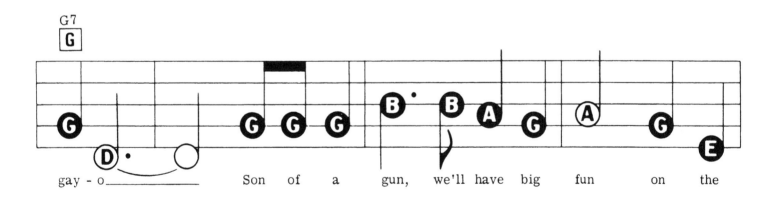

gay - o_____ Son of a gun, we'll have big fun on the

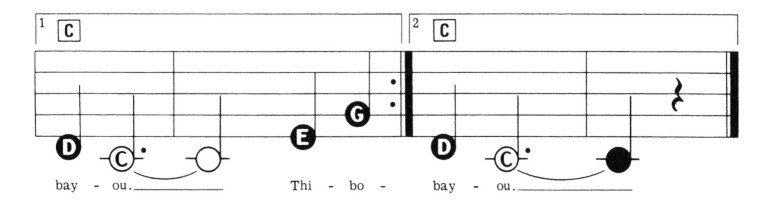

bay - ou._____ Thi - bo - bay - ou._____

King of the Road

Registration 7
Rhythm: Country

Words and Music by
Roger Miller

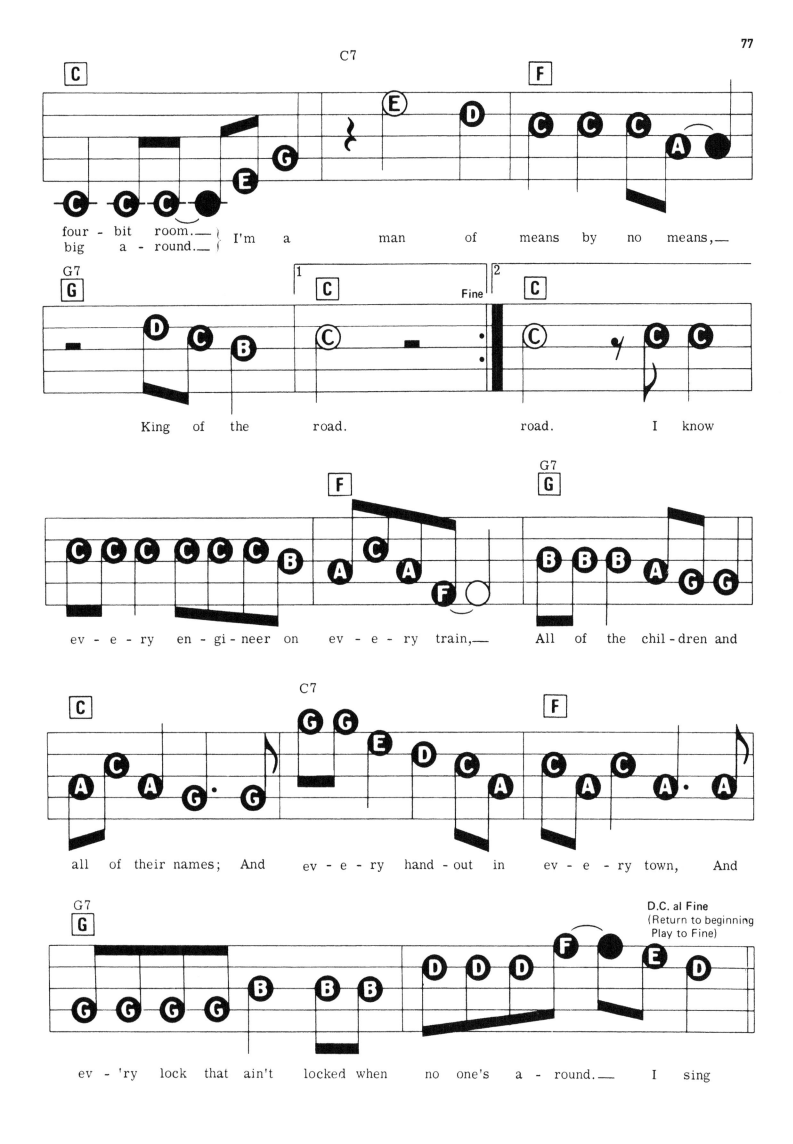

The Last Word in Lonesome Is Me

Registration 8
Rhythm: Waltz

Words and Music by
Roger Miller

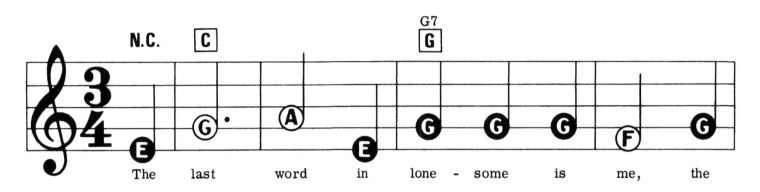

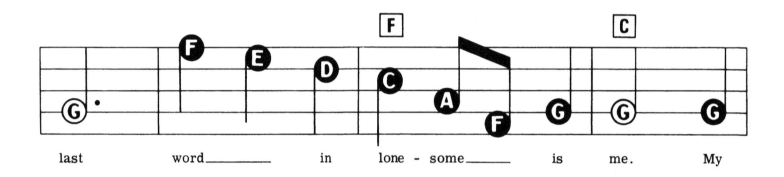

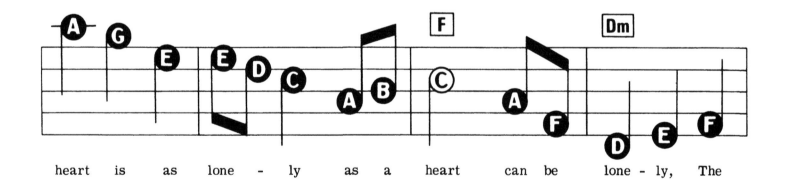

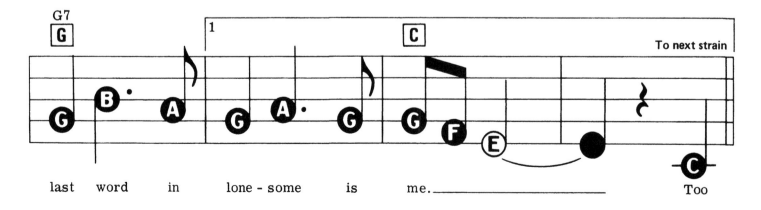

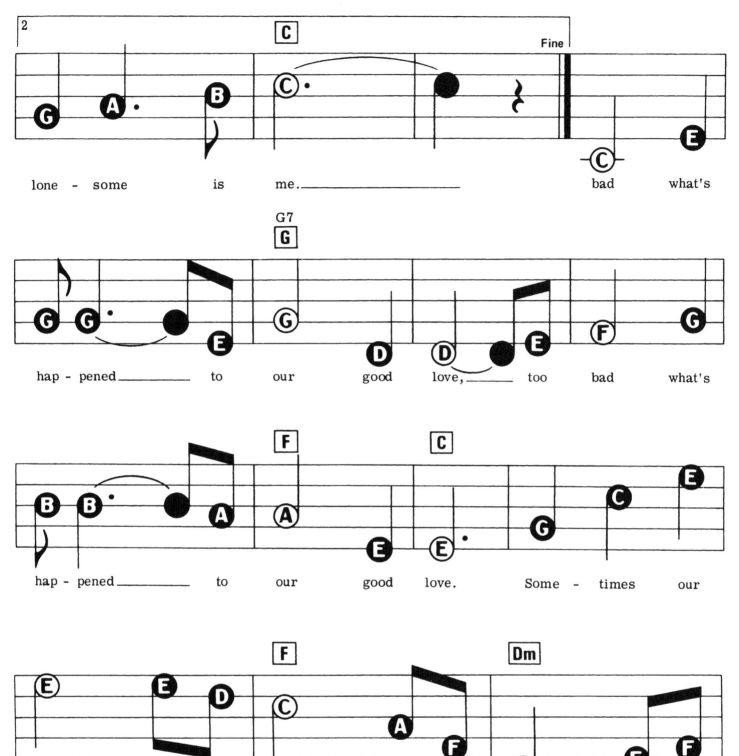

lone - some   is   me._____   bad   what's

hap - pened_____   to   our   good   love,_____   too   bad   what's

hap - pened_____   to   our   good   love.   Some - times   our

best   is - n't   quite   good   e - nough,   and   the

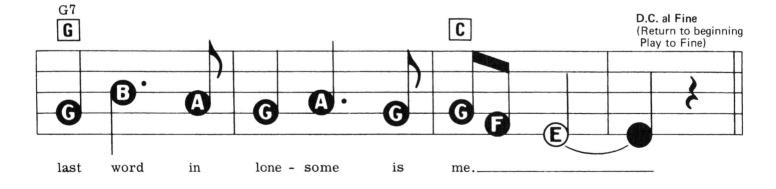

last   word   in   lone - some   is   me._____

Make the World Go Away

Registration 10
Rhythm: Country

Words and Music by
Hank Cochran

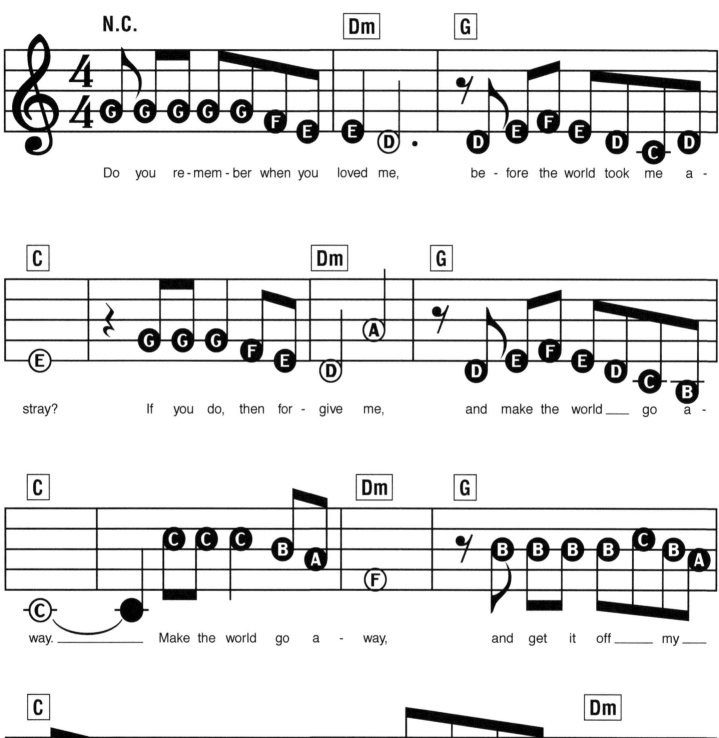

Do you re-mem-ber when you loved me, be-fore the world took me a-

stray? If you do, then for-give me, and make the world ___ go a-

way. _____ Make the world go a-way, and get it off _____ my ___

shoul-ders. Say the things you used to say,

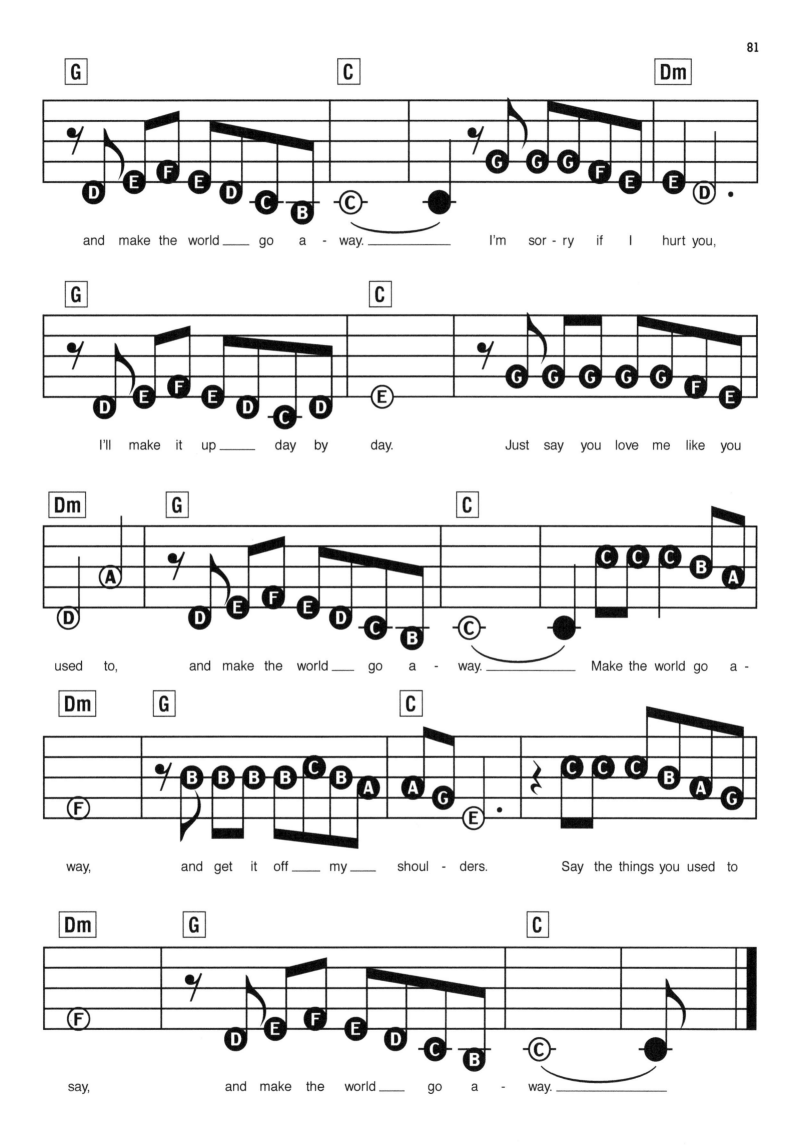

Mama Tried

Registration 7
Rhythm: Rock or Country

Words and Music by
Merle Haggard

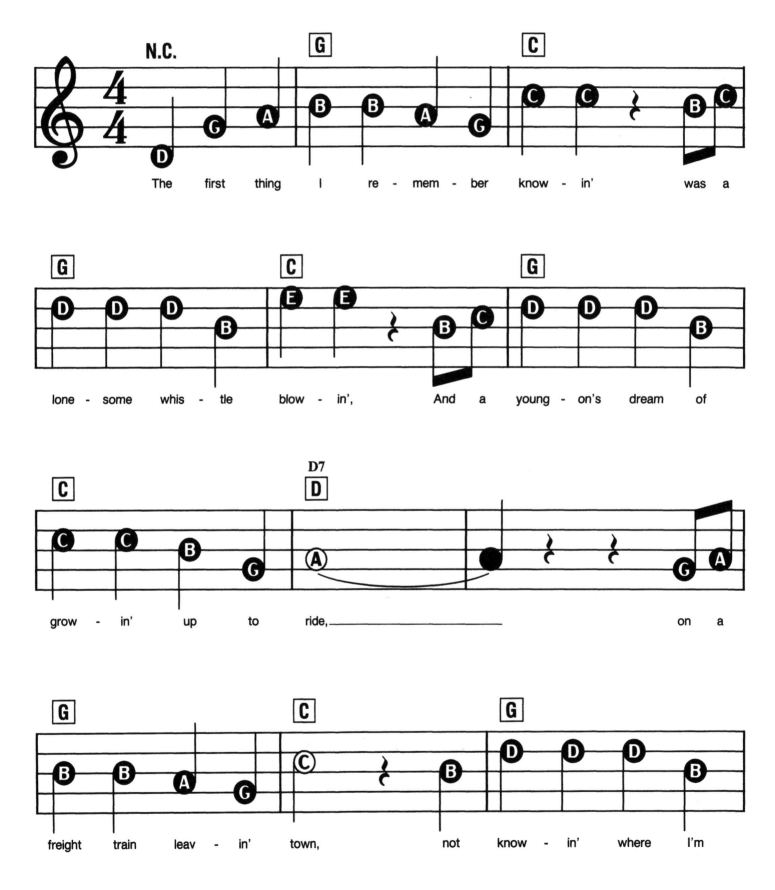

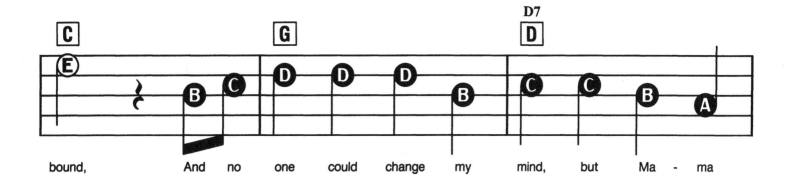

bound, And no one could change my mind, but Ma - ma

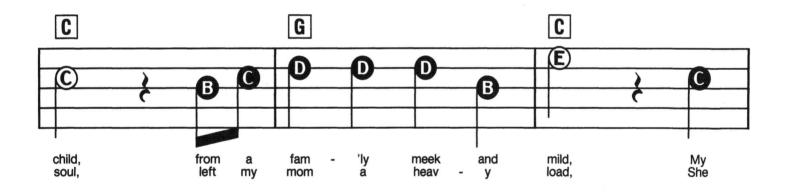

tried._____ One and
    on - ly reb - el
    dad - dy, rest his

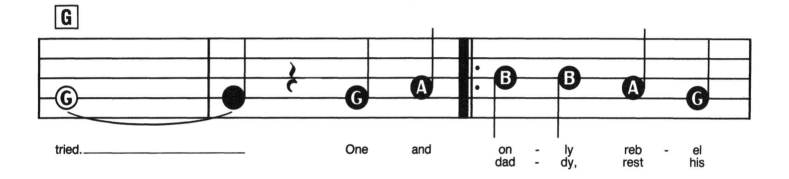

child, from a fam - 'ly meek and mild, My
soul, left my mom a heav - y load, She

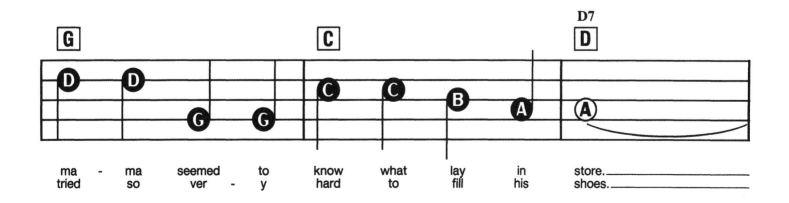

ma - ma seemed to know what lay in store._____
tried so ver - y hard to fill his shoes._____

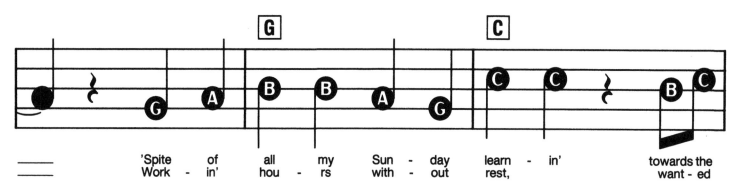

'Spite of all my Sun - day learn - in' towards the
Work - in' hou - rs with - out rest, want - ed

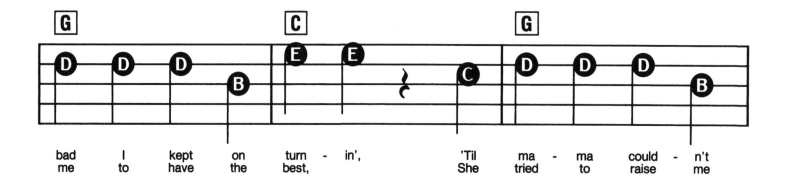

bad I kept on turn - in', 'Til ma - ma could - n't
me to have the best, She tried to raise me

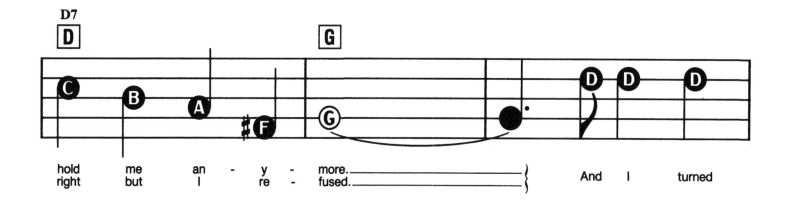

hold me an - y - more._____ And I turned
right me but I re - fused._____

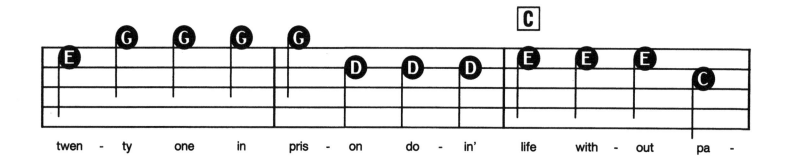

twen - ty one in pris - on do - in' life with - out pa -

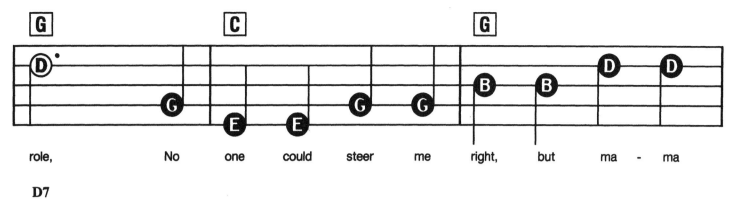

role, No one could steer me right, but ma - ma

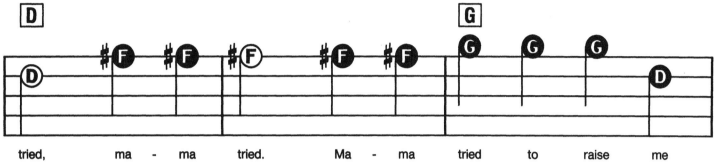

tried, ma - ma tried. Ma - ma tried to raise me

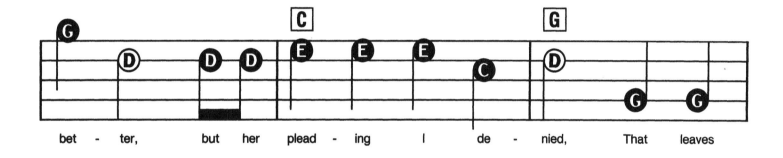

bet - ter, but her plead - ing I de - nied, That leaves

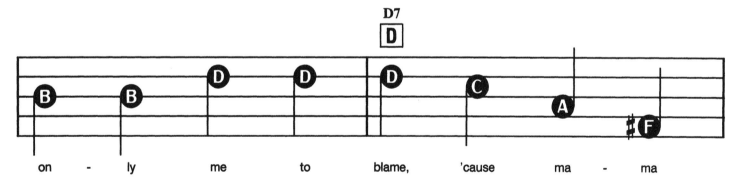

on - ly me to blame, 'cause ma - ma

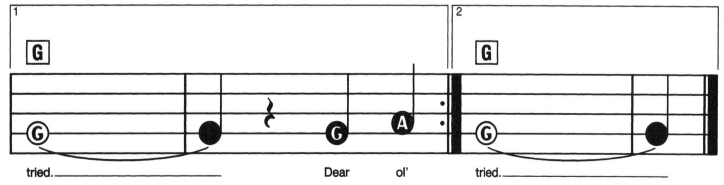

tried._____ Dear ol' tried._____

Mammas Don't Let Your Babies Grow Up to Be Cowboys

Registration 2
Rhythm: Waltz

Words and Music by Ed Bruce
and Patsy Bruce

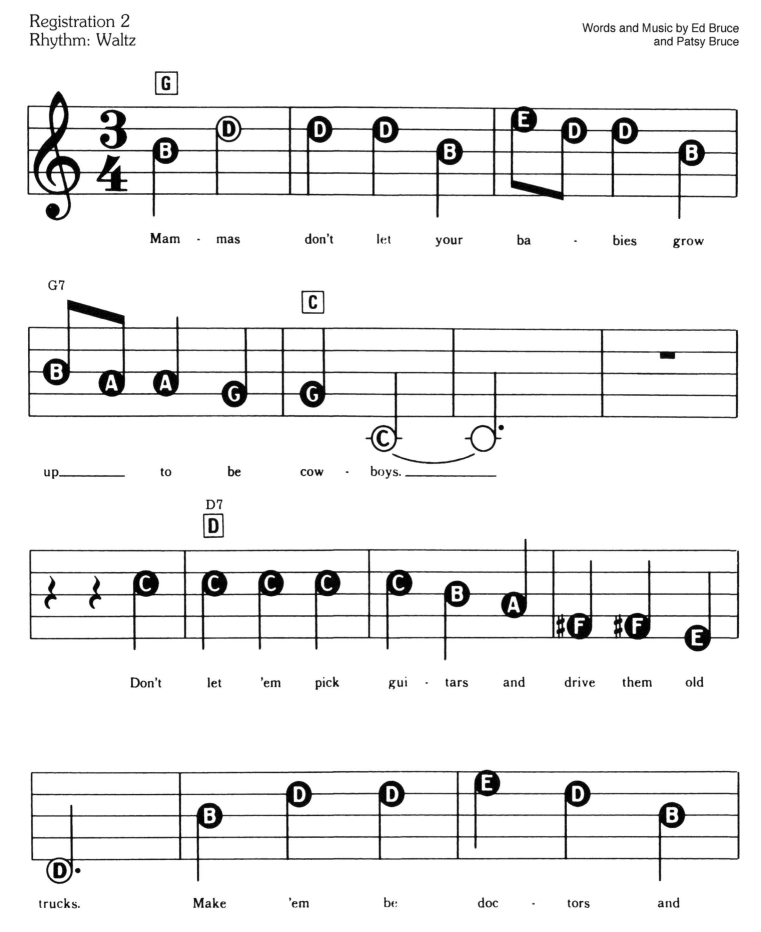

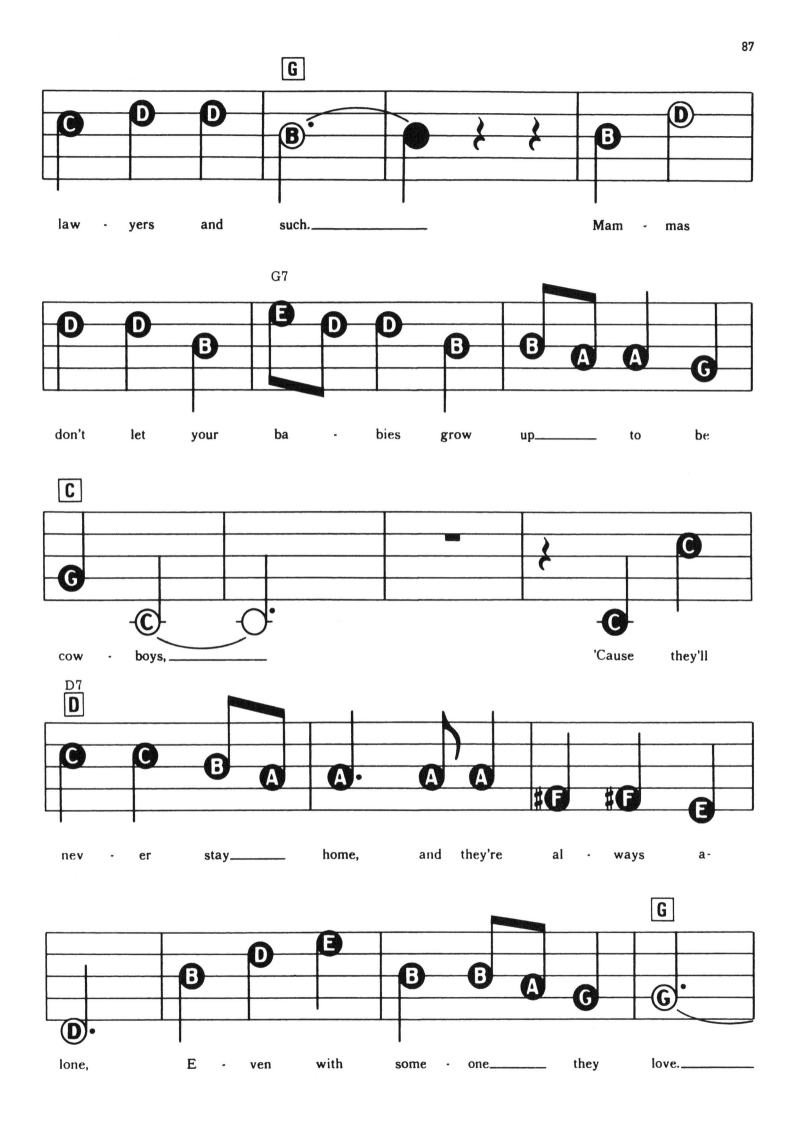

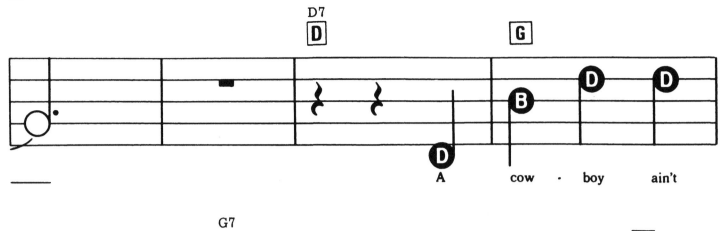

_____ A cow · boy ain't

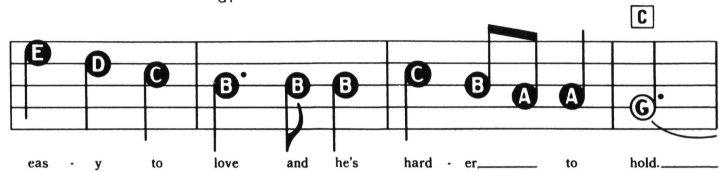

eas · y to love and he's hard · er_____ to hold._____

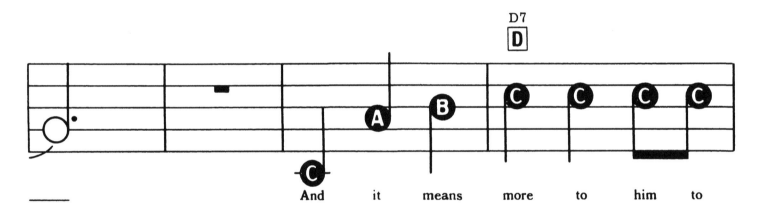

_____ And it means more to him to

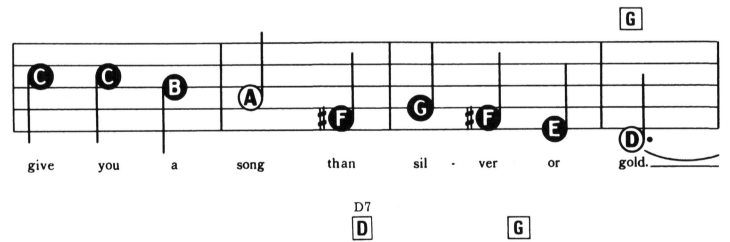

give you a song than sil · ver or gold._____

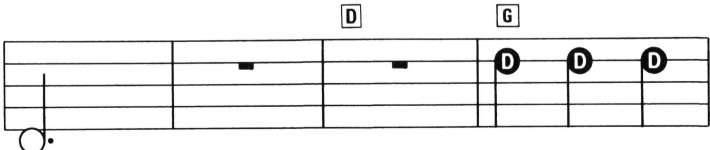

_____ Bud · wei · ser

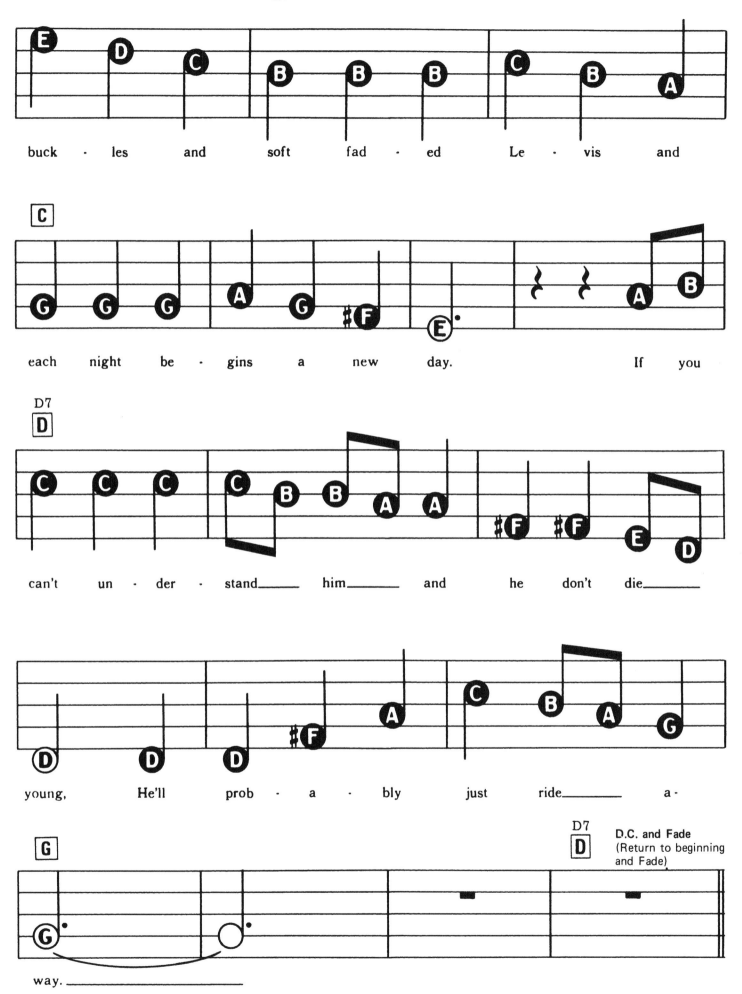

Mountain Music

Registration 3
Rhythm: Country or Shuffle

Words and Music by
Randy Owen

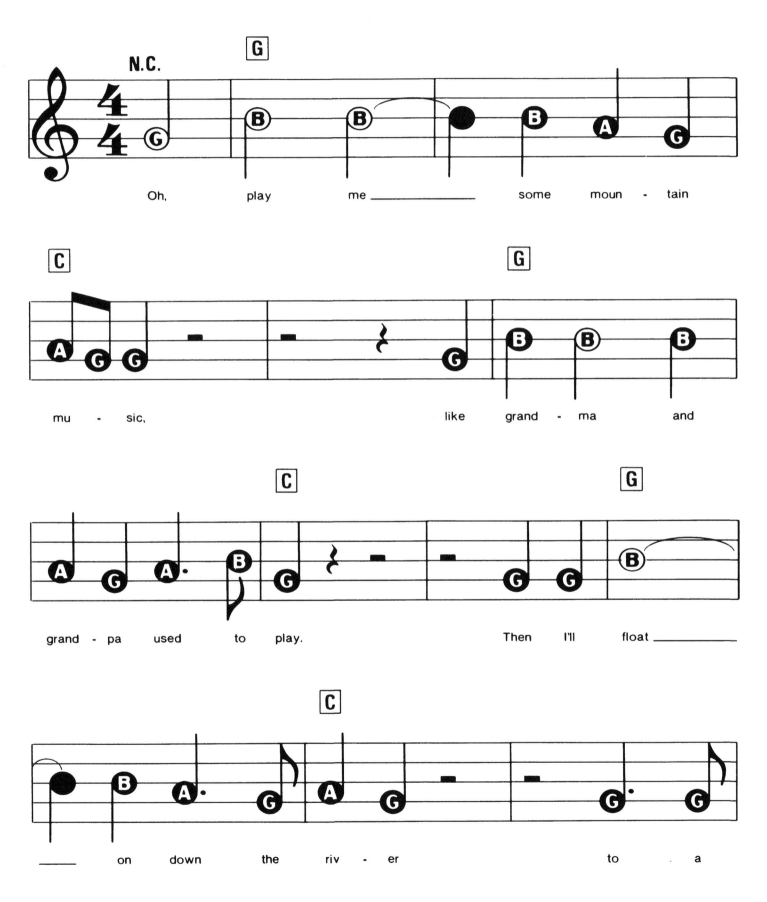

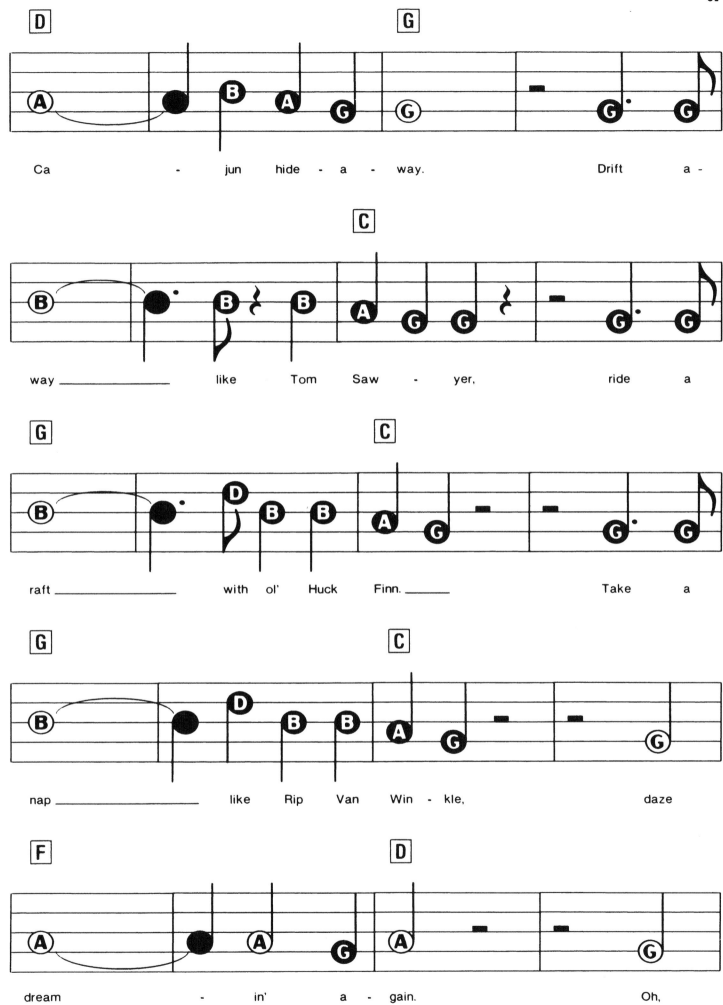

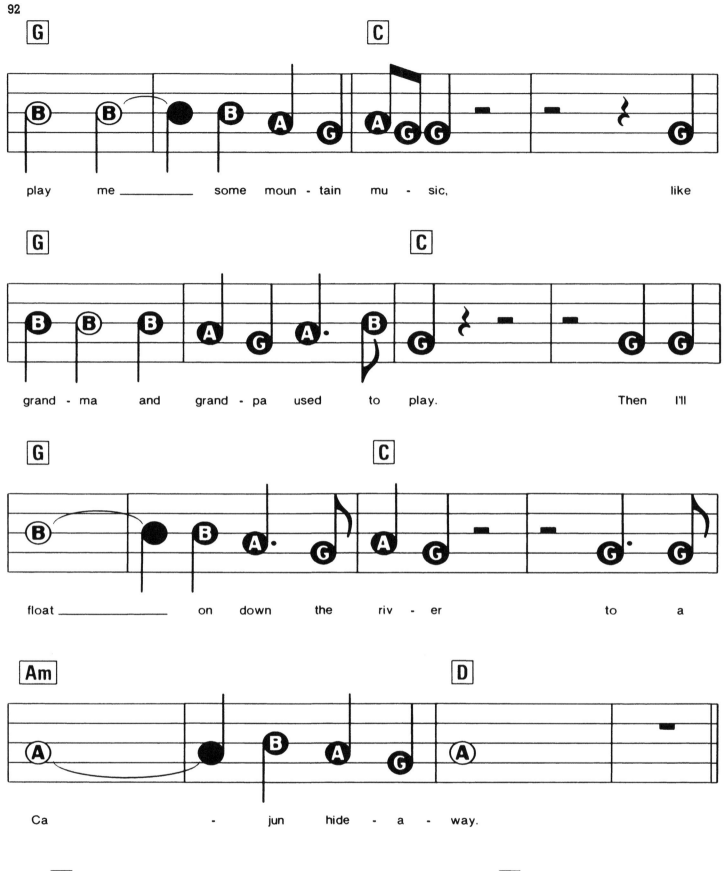

play   me _____ some moun - tain mu - sic,   like

grand - ma and grand - pa used to play.   Then I'll

float _____ on down the riv - er   to a

Ca   -   jun hide - a - way.

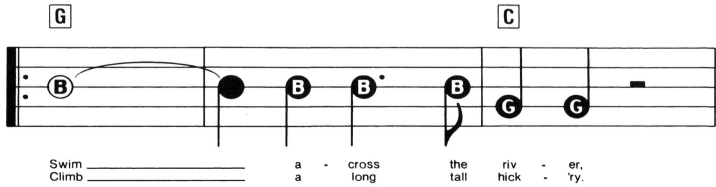

Swim _____   a - cross   the   riv - er,
Climb _____   a   long   tall hick - 'ry.

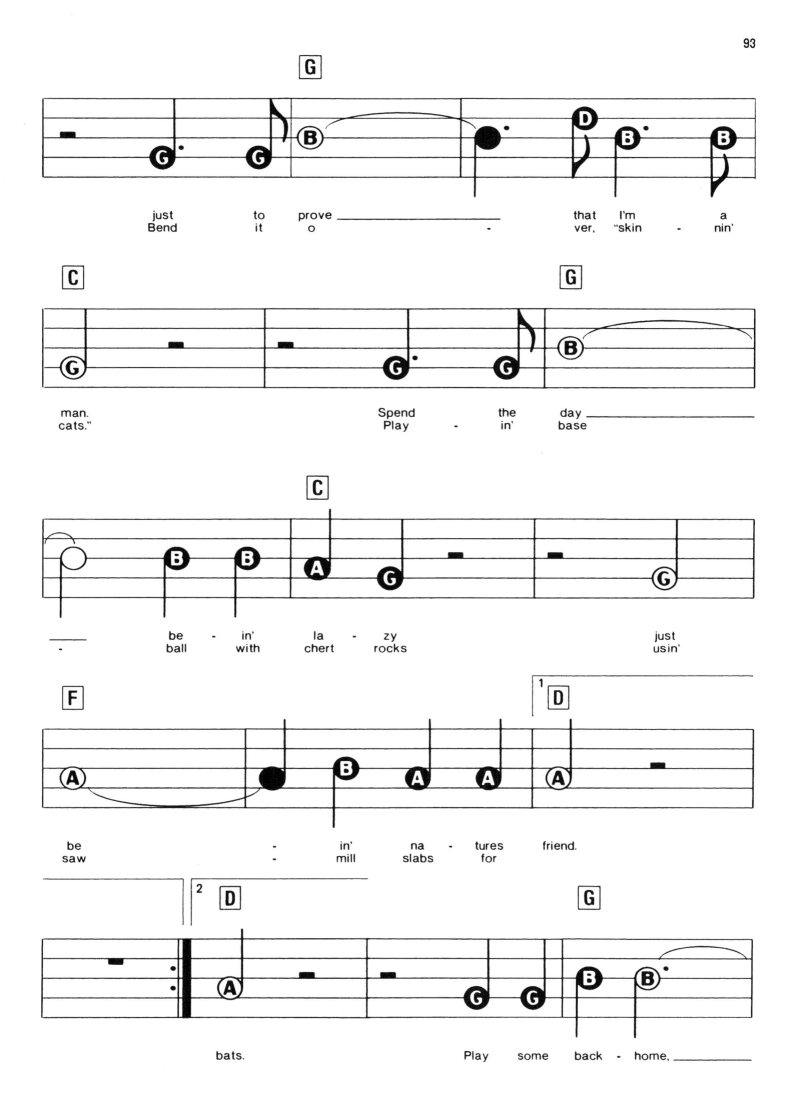

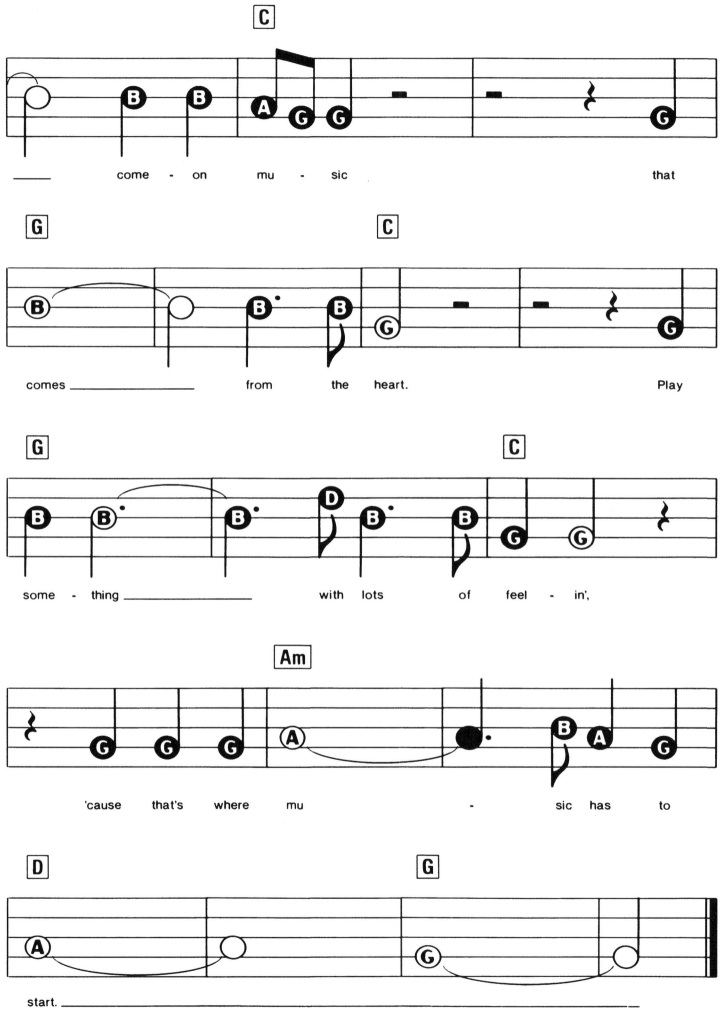

Okie from Muskogee

Registration 4
Rhythm: Country or Shuffle

Words and Music by Merle Haggard
and Roy Edward Burris

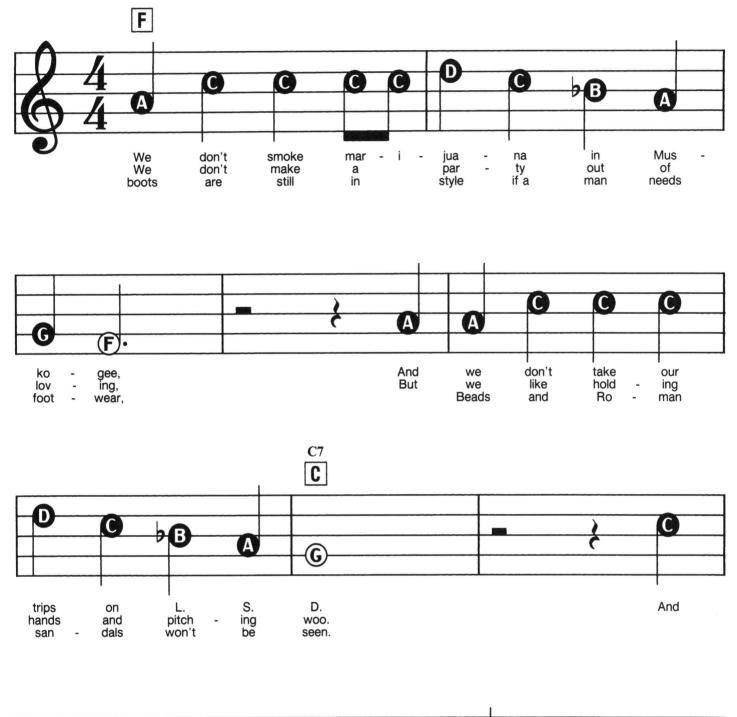

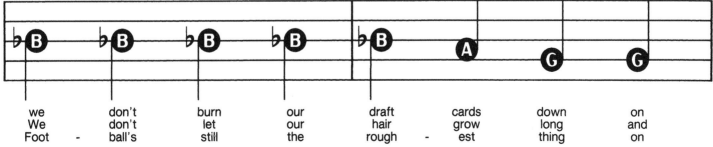

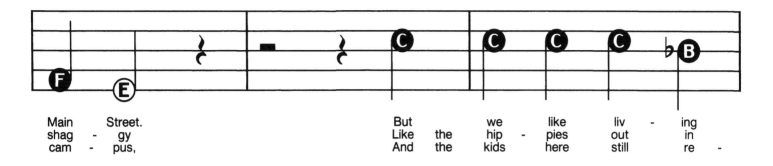

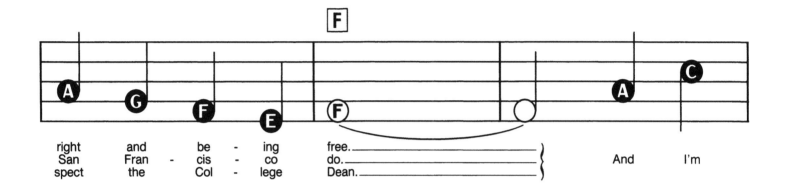

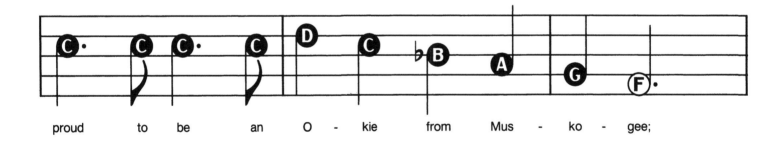

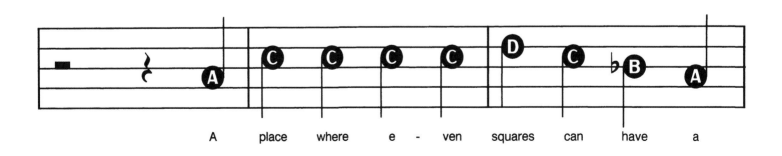

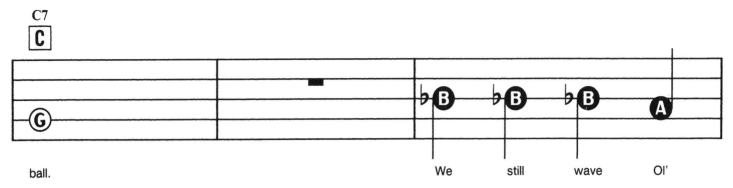

ball.   We   still   wave   Ol'

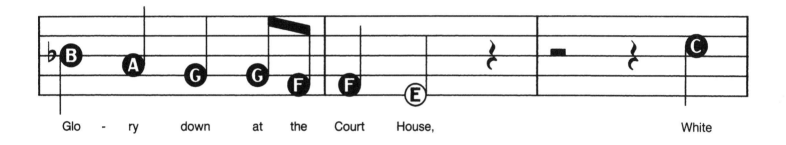

Glo - ry   down   at   the   Court   House,   White

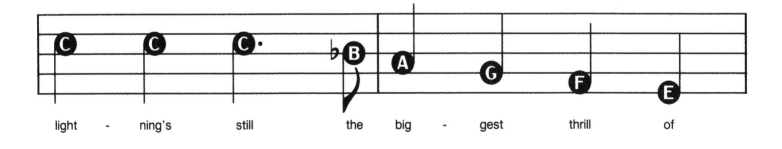

light - ning's   still   the   big - gest   thrill   of

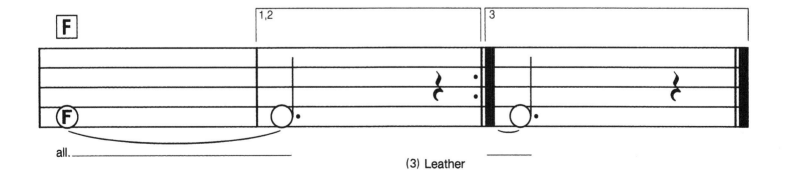

all.

(3) Leather

Oh, Lonesome Me

Registration 8
Rhythm: Country Shuffle or Country Swing

Words and Music by
Don Gibson

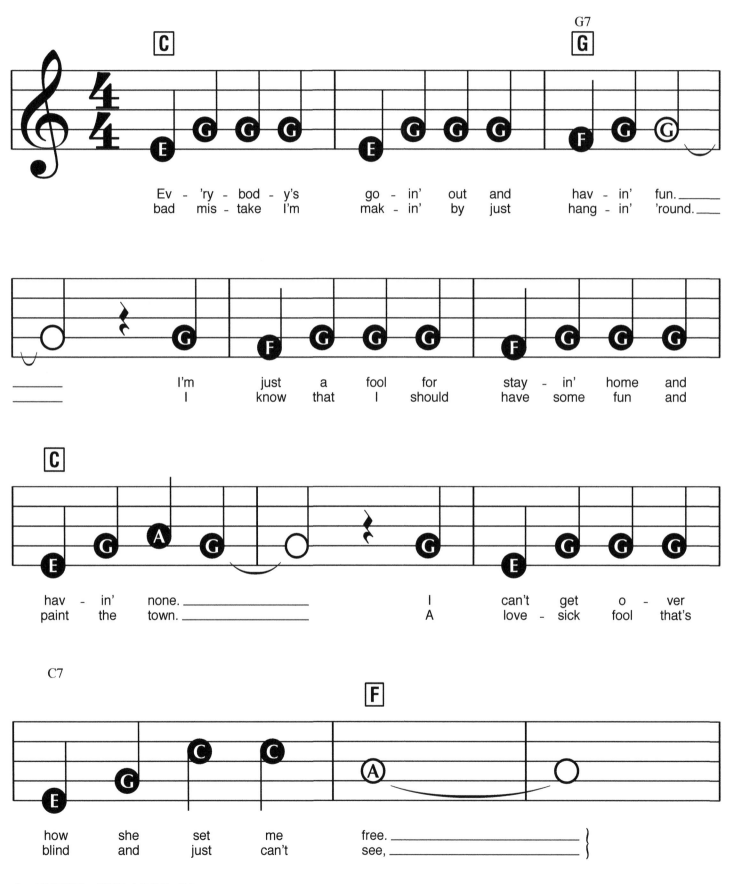

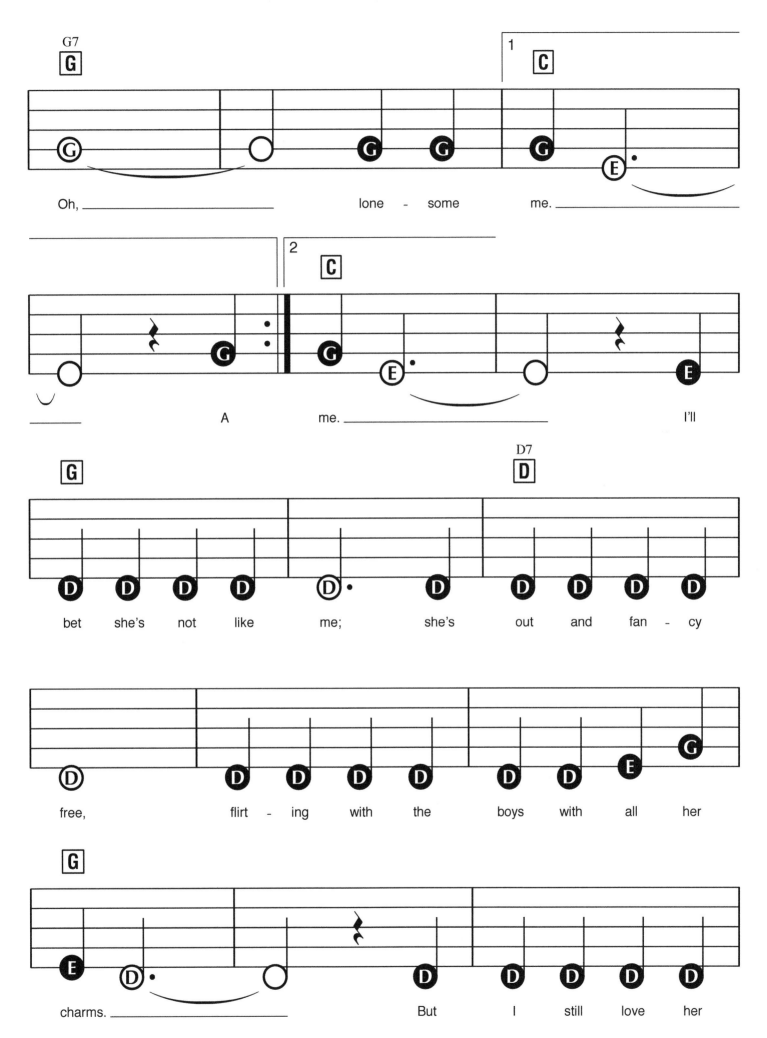

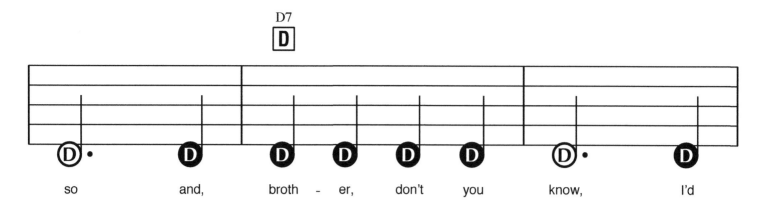

so and, broth - er, don't you know, I'd

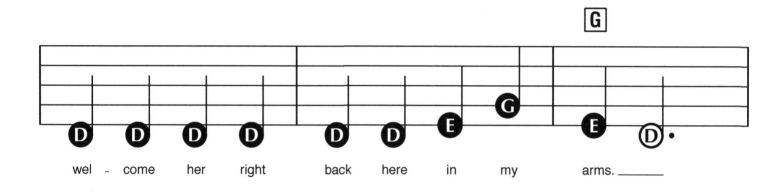

wel - come her right back here in my arms. _____

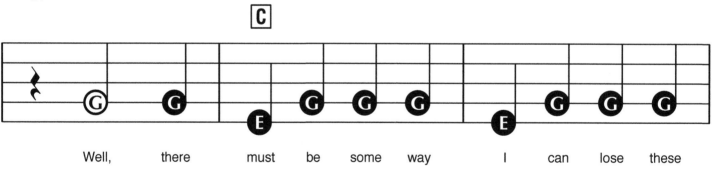

Well, there must be some way I can lose these

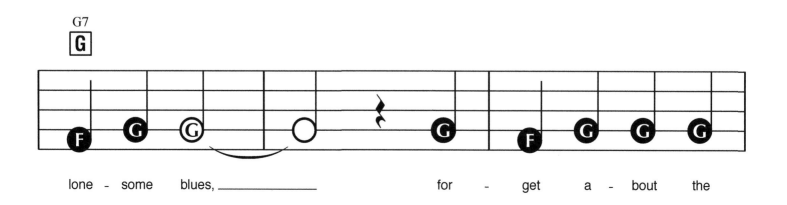

lone - some blues, _____ for - get a - bout the

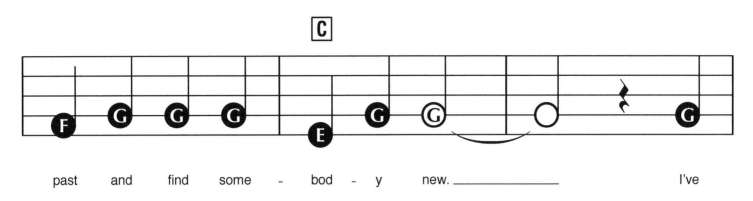

past and find some - bod - y new. _____ I've

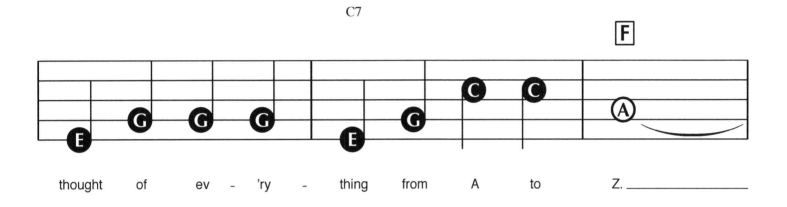

thought of ev - 'ry - thing from A to Z. _____

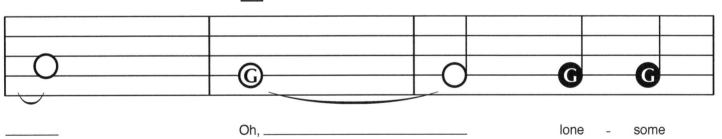

_____ Oh, _____ lone - some

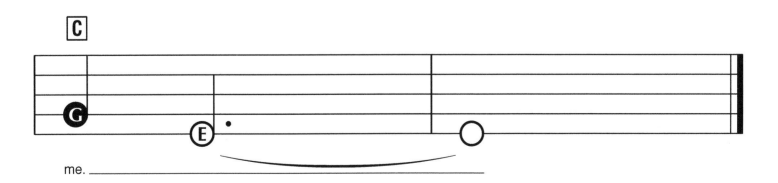

me. _____

Stand by Your Man

Registration 3
Rhythm: Country or Shuffle

Words and Music by Tammy Wynette
and Billy Sherrill

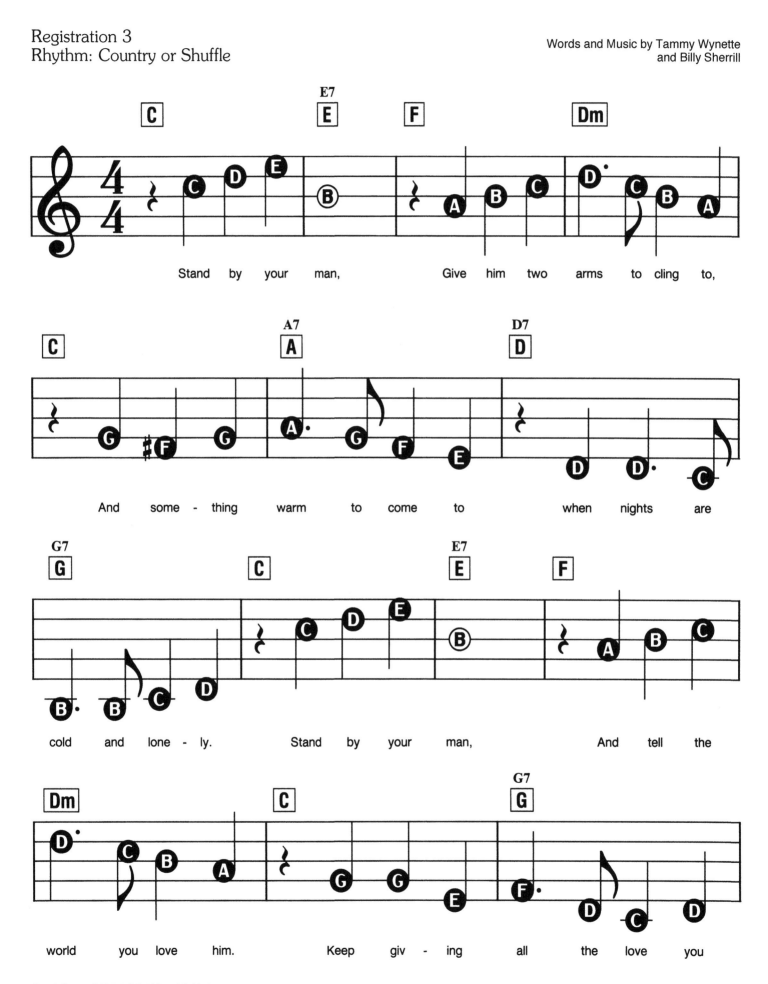

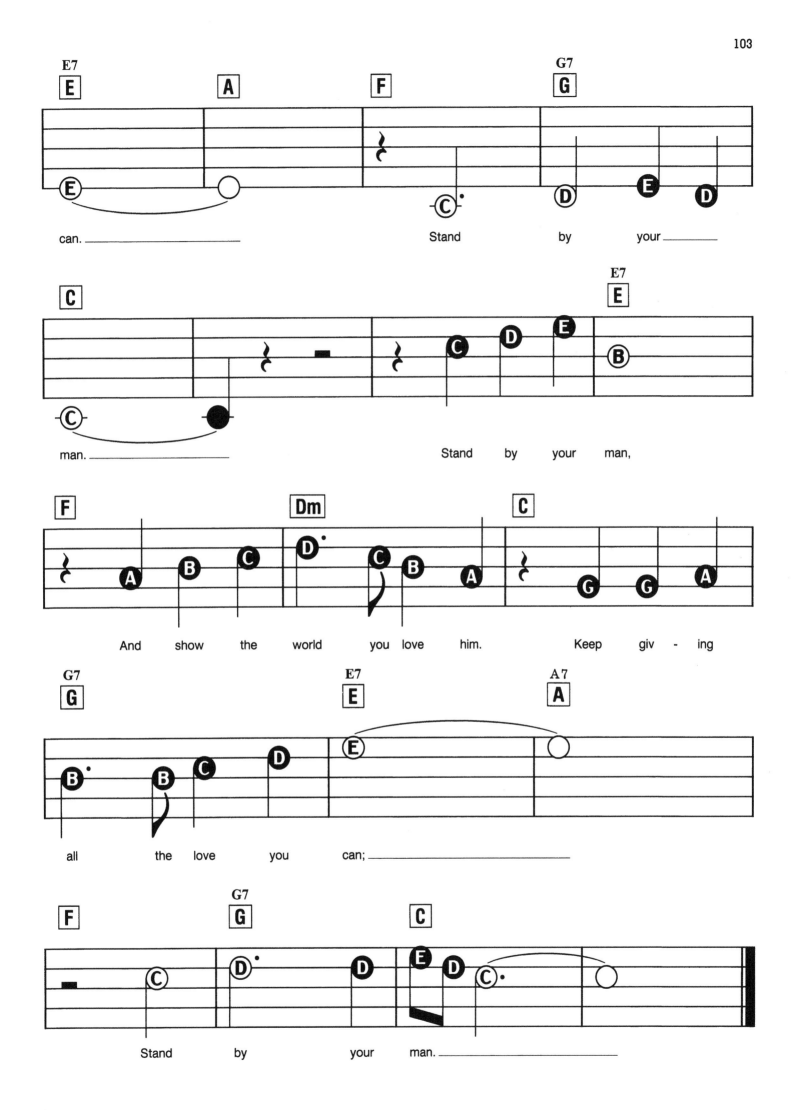

Tennessee Waltz

Registration 4
Rhythm: Waltz

Words and Music by Redd Stewart
and Pee Wee King

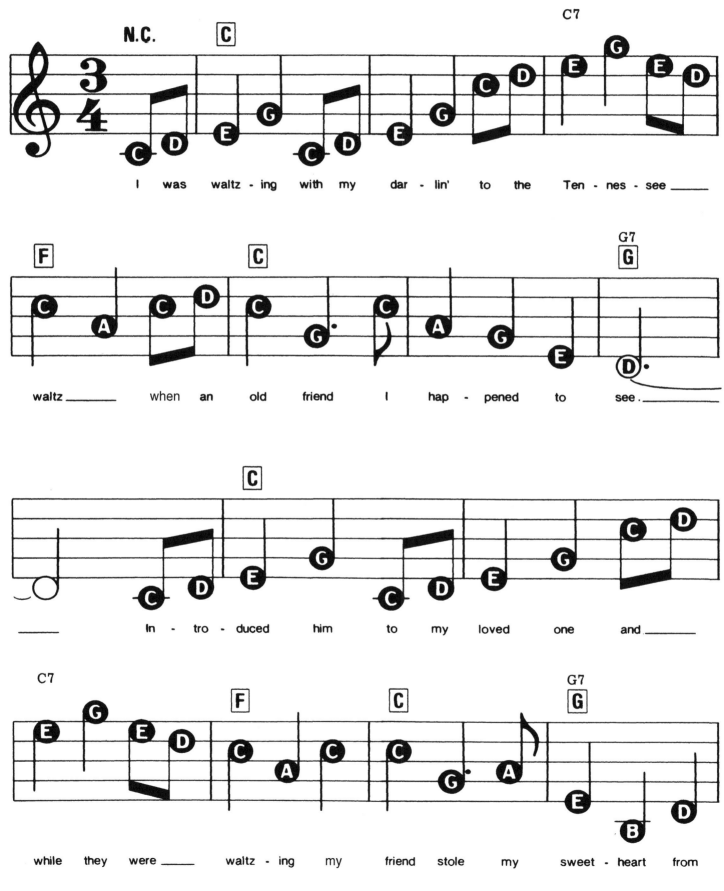

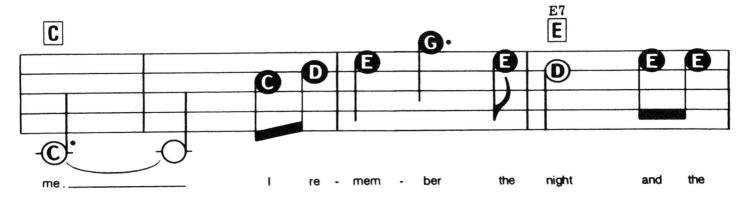

me. _____ I re - mem - ber the night and the

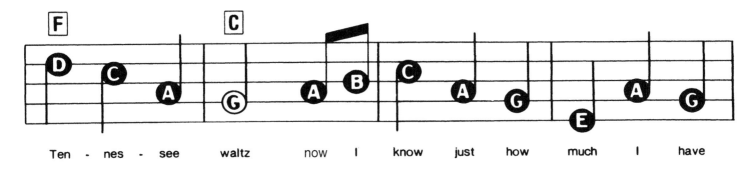

Ten - nes - see waltz now I know just how much I have

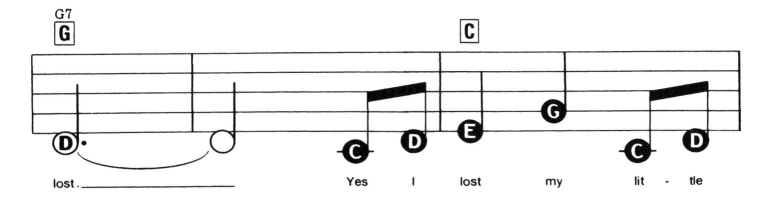

lost. _____ Yes I lost my lit - tle

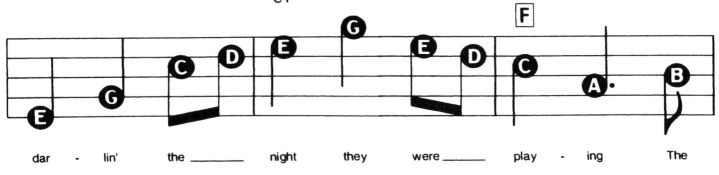

dar - lin' the _____ night they were _____ play - ing The

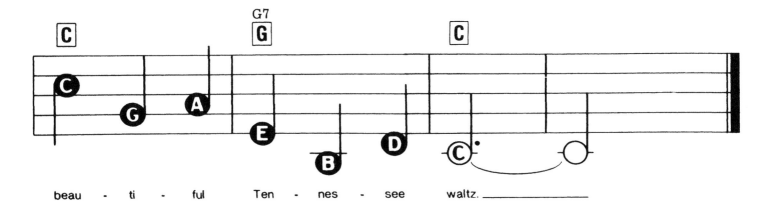

beau - ti - ful Ten - nes - see waltz. _____

Your Cheatin' Heart

Registration 4
Rhythm: Country or Swing

Words and Music by
Hank Williams

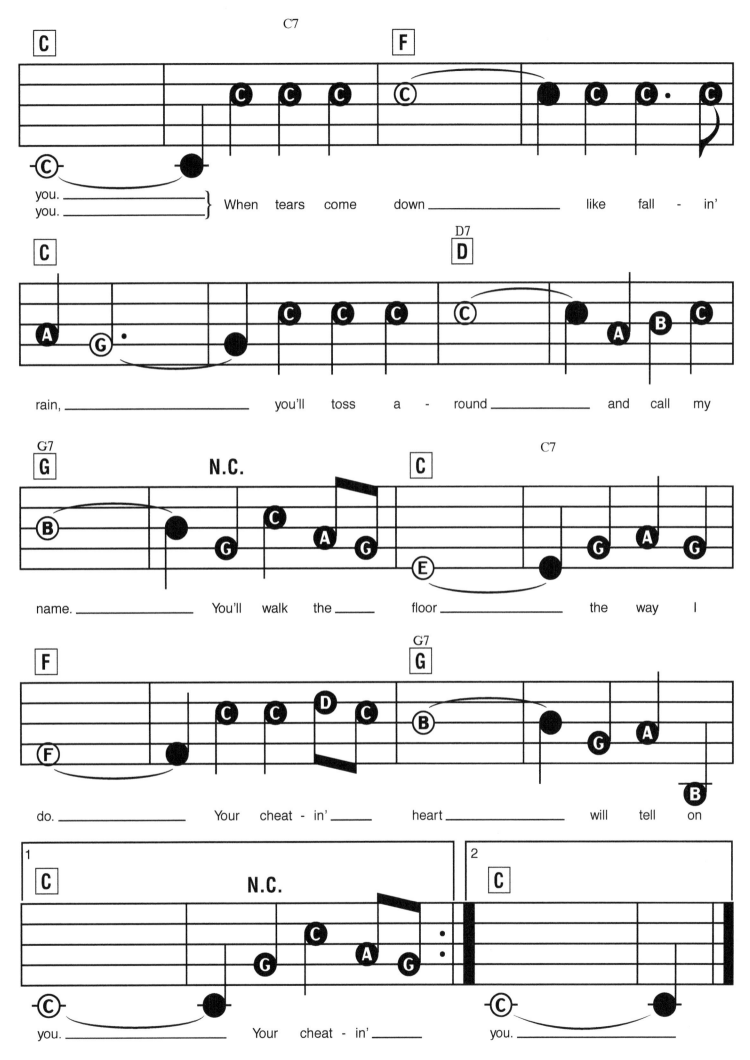

(Smooth As) Tennessee Whiskey

Registration 9
Rhythm: Country

Words and Music by Dean Dillon
and Linda Hargrove

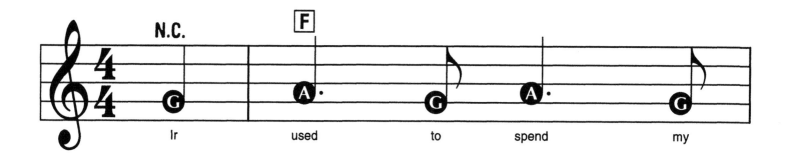

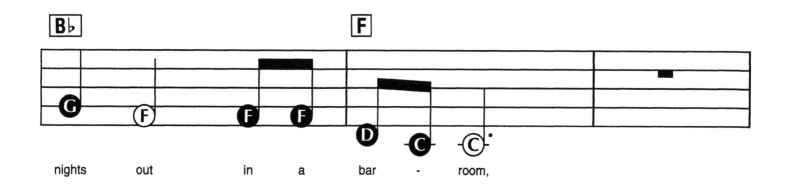

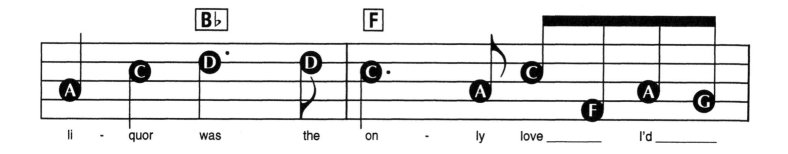

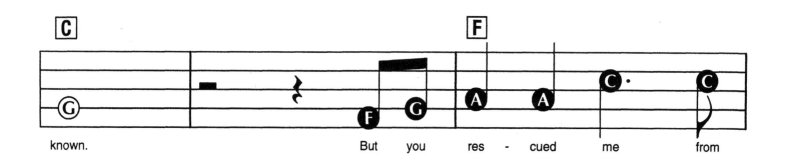

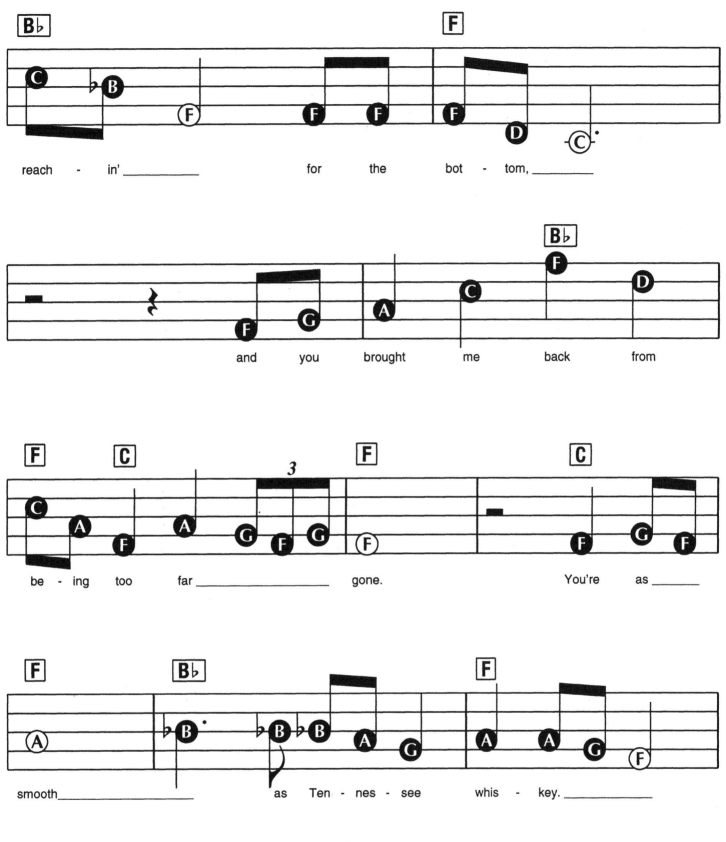

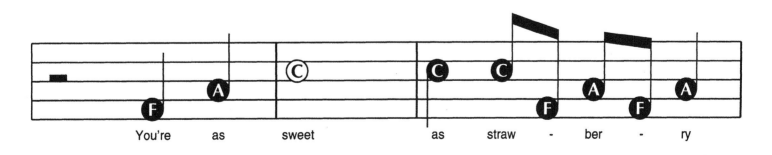

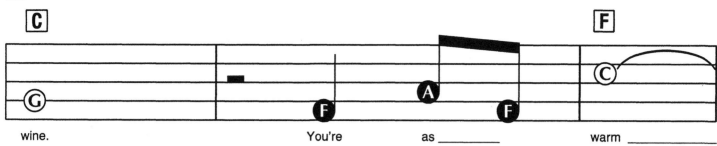

wine.   You're as _____ warm _____

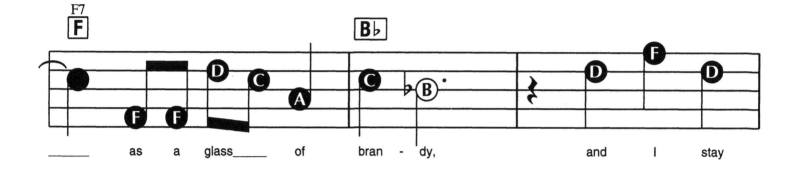

_____ as a glass____ of bran - dy,   and I stay

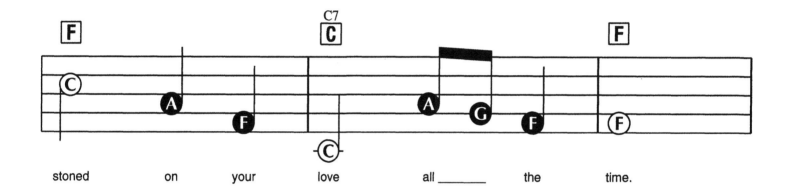

stoned on your love all _____ the time.

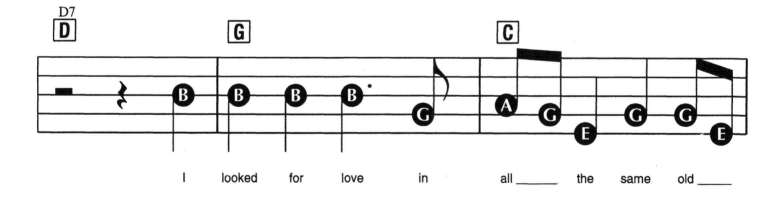

I looked for love in all _____ the same old _____

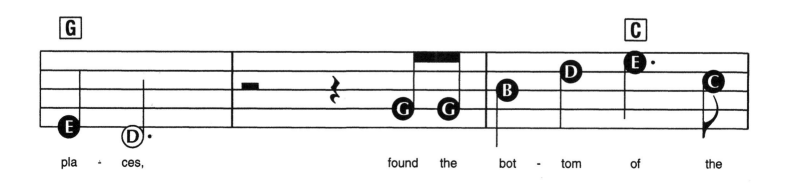

pla - ces,   found the bot - tom of the

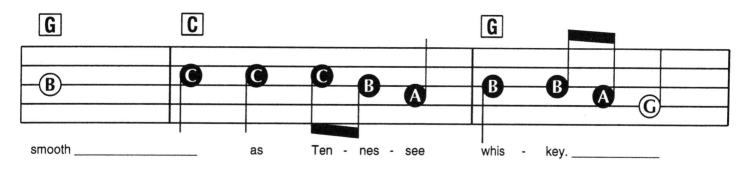

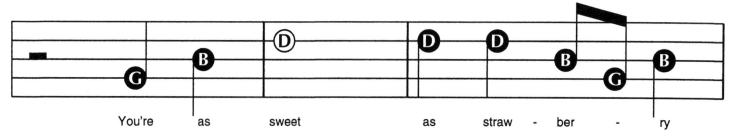

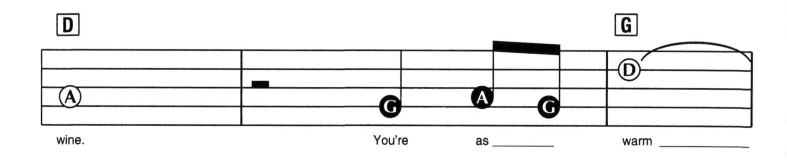

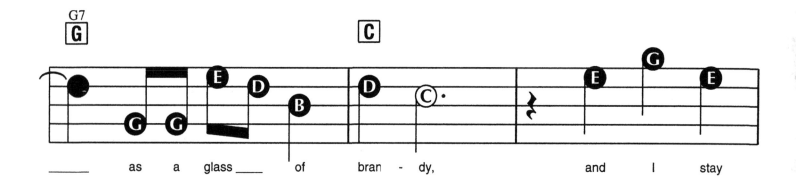

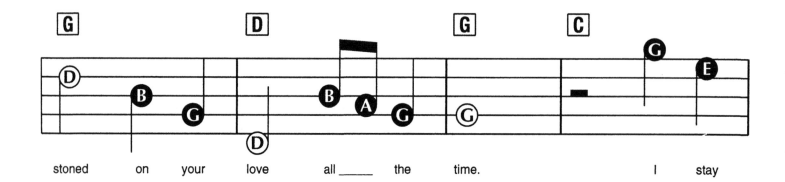

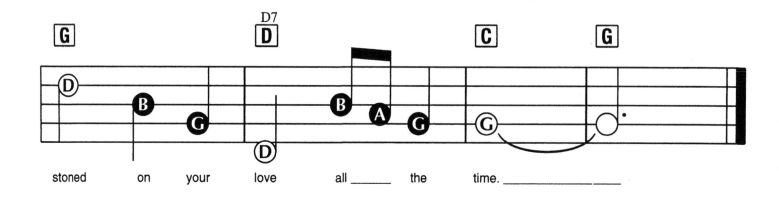